A SPECIAL EDITION FOR FRIENDS OF

PLANT CONSTRUCTION COMPANY, L.P.

The Mechanics' Institute of San Francisco was founded by pioneer craftsmen more than 150 years ago during the boom-and-bust times of the California gold rush. It became the first technical school, lending and reference library and social center in the western United States freely open to men and women in the mechanical arts. In the ensuing years, while science and technology created phenomenal changes in communication, transportation, manufacturing and construction, the Mechanics' Institute remained a powerful advocate of technical education and economic development, while its bookshelves and reading rooms ripened into a rich general library. Plant Construction Company is pleased to have the privilege of introducing the Mechanics' Institute to those of our clients and friends who are not already acquainted with this unique cultural and educational institution.

FOUR BOOKS 300 DOLLARS AND A DREAM

An Illustrated History of the First 150 Years of the Mechanics' Institute of San Francisco

HOW A PIONEER READING ROOM
FOR THE EDUCATION OF CRAFTSMEN
BECAME A MAJOR LIBRARY, RESEARCH
FACILITY AND SOCIAL CENTER IN
THE HEART OF A BUSY CITY

RICHARD REINHARDT

MECHANICS' INSTITUTE
SAN FRANCISCO · 2005

MECHANICS' INSTITUTE
LIBRARY & CHESS ROOM

Published by Mechanics' Institute,
57 Post Street, San Francisco, CA 94104
Membership and inquiries: www.milibrary.org

LCCN: 2005937450
ISBN: 0-9776435-0-6

Most of the historic photographs and drawings in this
book are from the archives of the Mechanics' Institute.
Additional illustrations have been reproduced from
the author's collection and through the courtesy of
the Bancroft Library, University of California, Berkeley:
pp. 24, 31 (top), 63 (top), 66, 67; the California Historical
Society: pp. 27 (top), 33 (left), 34 (bottom), 35, 43 (bottom);
History Center, San Francisco Public Library: pp. 2,
26 (bottom), 28 (center), 29, 33 (right), 45 (bottom), 46, 49 (top),
51 (left), 62, 63 (bottom), 69 (top), 72, 87, 90 (bottom left), 103;
National Portrait Gallery of Great Britain: p. 7;
San Francisco Architectural Heritage: pp. 74 (bottom), 78;
and San Francisco Performing Arts Library & Museum:
pp. 11, 36. The endpapers, second frontispiece (p. viii),
back cover and pp. 107–116 are by Ken Newman.
The main title pages and pp. 92 and 93 are by Pirkle Jones.

FRONT COVER IMAGE Setting the cornerstone of
the current building at 57 Post Street, 1909.

BACK COVER IMAGE The entrance to the Mechanics' Institute, 2005.

TITLE PAGE The circular stairwell of 57 Post Street, 1955.

SPONSORS

The publication of this book has been supported by a generous grant from

THE CANDELARIA FUND

And by the kind assistance of

RICHARD LAIDERMAN & JUNG-WHA SONG
GLADYS G. MOORE
MARK & LISA PINTO
JOHN WILEY & SONS, INC.
PETER BOOTH WILEY

---

*The Mechanics' Institute also gratefully acknowledges the contributions of
members and friends who helped make the publication of this book possible*

Bruce D. Celebrezze, Jim Friedman &
Suzanne Stassevitch, Charles W. Kenady,
the Honorable Tomar Mason, Susan Mulvey & Mark Temple

Jane & Oliver Bryk, Neil & Barbara Falconer, Jim & Betsy Flack,
Wanda L. Fluallen—in memory of Joseph B. Fluallen,
David & Stella Goodwin, David J. Madson, Vincent E. McCambridge,
Rosemary & Robert Gray Patton, Jerome L. Stark

David A. Abercrombie, Anonymous (1), Adele Engel Behar,
Richard Hosmer Adams Blum, Inez & Hal Cohen, Robert & Barbara DeMaria,
Thomas Rex Hardy, Donald F. Hodges, Marge Mayne, Theodor Schuchat, John Sims

The Mechanics' Institute gratefully acknowledges the following
people who supported the Sesquicentennial mid-year appeal

CONTENTS

―――――――

FOREWORD
BY KEVIN STARR
ix

ACKNOWLEDGMENTS
xi

An Illustrated History of the First 150 Years
of the Mechanics' Institute of San Francisco

A RESPECT FOR LEARNING
AND THE LIFE OF THE MIND...

IN PREPARING this elegantly researched, written, and designed history of the Mechanics' Institute of San Francisco, Richard Reinhardt has achieved a new history of San Francisco itself; for the institution he chronicles was at the core of a number of identities and aspirations that transformed a ramshackle, haphazard frontier town into a city of world renown. The Mechanics' Institute embodied a major ambition of mid-nineteenth-century America: the desire of working people to continue their educations through reading, lectures, discussions, and related forms of self-improvement. This desire for a better life, a better identity, on the part of working men and women fed directly into their ambition to create a city in the fullest sense of that term on the edge of a near-empty half-continent.

The Mechanics' Institute movement, as Reinhardt documents, had its origins in Edinburgh, Scotland, in 1821 and came quickly across the Atlantic to Philadelphia and New York, where it dovetailed with the Mercantile Library model that can be traced back to the Library Company founded by Benjamin Franklin in 1731. This Scots-American connection is not surprising. Immigrants of Scots descent had peopled North America in the eighteenth century; the thinkers of the Edinburgh-based Scottish Enlightenment exercised a decisive influence on the development of Colonial American political theory, leading directly to the Declaration of Independence and the Constitution.

At the core of this sensibility was a respect for learning and the life of the mind and, of equal importance, a respect for the individual, whatever his or her social circumstances. The word *mechanic*, as Walt Whitman would understand and celebrate this word by the 1840s, was not merely someone who worked with his or her hands, important as that might be. A *mechanic* was a skilled maker of things, an avid student of technology, a self-respecting yeoman eager to make his way in the world and the

woman, in many instances, who accompanied him on this journey and shared his skills. Thus, the mechanic was the maker, the artisan, *homo faber*, man the fabricator, as the Romans would put it, or, from the perspective of ancient Greece, the master of *techne*, technique, be that *techne* the design of a temple, the sculpture of a statue, the construction of a house, the repair of a cart, or the joining of wood to stone to create a bench. The frontier San Francisco photographer Carleton Watkins, among others, saw himself as a working man, a mechanic, employing the tools of his trade to capture accurate and well-positioned images; such a lack of pretense, such a concern for foundational skills, whatever the project, was characteristic of his fellow mechanics in a variety of callings. In his poetry, Walt Whitman celebrated such mechanics, so ready to apply their skills to American life; and while the professors of Europe in their well-appointed laboratories struggled with the challenges of technological breakthrough, such American mechanics as Robert Fulton, Cyrus McCormick, Samuel F. B. Morse, Alexander Graham Bell, Lester Allen Pelton, and the Wright brothers achieved breakthroughs in the steamboat, the mechanical reaper, the telegraph, the telephone, the hydraulic wheel, and heavier-than-air flight that constituted the major technological innovations of the nineteenth and early twentieth centuries.

Far from limiting themselves, the pioneers who came to San Francisco with the gold rush and founded the Mechanics' Institute in 1854 were celebrating themselves as Americans ready to remake themselves through self-instruction, to make things with their hands, to celebrate the results of their artistry in a great pavilion in the course of annual exhibitions, and, by doing what they were doing, to play their role in the larger task of making nothing less than a city, one of the highest forms of human achievement.

THE DONAHUE MONUMENT at Bush, Battery and Market Streets (Douglas Tilden, 1899)
celebrates the contribution of mechanics to the creation and development of the city.

Like the Institute they founded, the San Francisco created by the mechanics of the city embodied thousands of years of human aspiration and achievement. Historians marvel at the overnight creation of San Francisco. So, too, might they marvel at the rapid creation of the Mechanics' Institute program: its collection of books (200,000 volumes by 1906) and periodicals; its annual exhibitions (including the Great Cheese of 1864, all 3936 pounds of it!); its connection to the state university, which linked it to research and higher education; the lecture podium it afforded the great and near-great of the era; the art it exhibited; the chess competitions it sponsored; the public library system it helped to create; its merger with the Mercantile Library; its destruction by earthquake and fire in 1906; and its rebuilding of itself thereafter for another century of service.

Here, then, unfolds the history of an Institute founded by mechanics. Here as well is the social and cultural history of the city they created as they went about their daily business: as they read and studied, argued the great issues of the day, and celebrated the results of their collective and individual industry. To read this history is once again to experience the perils and triumphs those founding mechanics experienced while building lives and building a city in a cascade of forward-flowing time. The Institute they created remains with us. And so does the city.

KEVIN STARR
California State Librarian Emeritus

ACKNOWLEDGMENTS

———

THE HISTORY of the Mechanics' Institute is scattered among many documents, photographs and publications, most of which are preserved in the archives of the Institute, along with a useful but sadly incomplete file of unpublished records of the Mercantile Association (1852–1906). All accounts of the founding and early development of the Institute are indebted for structure and details to Andrew S. Hallidie's unpublished "Story of the Mechanics' Institute" (1896); John H. Wood's *Seventy-Five Years of History of the Mechanics' Institute of San Francisco* (1930); and William G. Merchant's *100 Years of the Mechanics' Institute, 1855–1955* (1955).

In assembling this first illustrated history of an influential and enduring educational institution, the author has relied heavily on the energetic participation of Library Director Inez Shor Cohen at every stage of the project, in searching out and making available pictorial materials, reading and commenting on sections of the manuscript, and giving unstintingly of her time, advice and encouragement. The Library's photographic exhibit "After the Gold Rush," a project of the Sesquicentennial year, supplied essential research into the Institute's thirty-one industrial expositions.

Head Reference Librarian Craig Jackson and Reference Librarians Erika Schmidt and Mark André Singer have devoted valuable time and energy to ferreting out elusive facts and producing useable pictorial images out of scattered sources. International Master John Donaldson, a diligent historian as well as chess director, is responsible for whatever is accurate in the chess history, and not for the author's errors and omissions.

Many friends in allied cultural and educational institutions, and trustees, former trustees and staff members of the Institute have been generous with help: Don Andreini (San Francisco Architectural Heritage); Harvey Jones (Oakland Museum of California); Grand Master Nick de Firmian; Louise Frankel, Clark Maser and Robert Burger (former trustees); Michael Savage (building manager); Dipak Pallana (technical support); Neil Falconer and Mark Pinto (trustees and former presidents of the Institute); and, for constant enthusiastic support for this publication project, Executive Director Jim Flack.

RICHARD REINHARDT

OVERLEAF The second-floor reading room one morning in 2005.

A GOLDEN APPLE IN THE WORLD'S EYE

SAN FRANCISCO began as a scattering of tribal villages, built of mud and wattles on the rich brown tide flats of a vast and isolated inland bay. In 1776 an expedition of soldiers, priests and would-be settlers arrived on the shore after a 1500-mile trek from Mexico and set up a military and religious colony on behalf of the king of Spain. This lonely little outpost endured for seven decades on a simple, two-way trade in cattle hides, seal fur and lumber, swapping its local products for shoes and combs, buttons and mirrors from Boston, wine and oil from Spain. Throughout those years, the settlement consisted of little more than a small army post, a Catholic mission and a village of adobe houses, shops and storage sheds on a shallow cove called Yerba Buena—"good herb"—for the wild mint flowering on the nearby hills. San Francisco was the farthest reach, the last fingerhold of the overextended Spanish empire.

FRANK MARRYAT'S FAMOUS CARTOON of San Franciscans wallowing along the waterfront in "The Winter of 1849" appeared in his satirical *Mountains and Molehills* (1855).

Toward the middle of the nineteenth century, two unrelated events brought San Francisco suddenly to the attention of the world. First, the young American nation, stretching westward across the Mississippi Valley, developed an urge to reach from sea to sea and sent its army and navy in 1846 to capture Texas, California and the other northern provinces of Mexico. Then, less than two years after American troops had secured the territory, a highly publicized discovery of precious yellow metal in the Sierra foothills set off one of the greatest human migrations in history, the gold rush to California.

The image of San Francisco during the gold rush years is deeply engraved—and somewhat exaggerated—in the American mind. In this fanciful picture, San Francisco is the ultimate frontier harbor, glittering with promises of sudden wealth and high adventure. In a few chaotic years, the little Mexican village is transformed into a rowdy city of fifty or sixty thousand adventurers. Its shallow cove, with its unpronounceable Spanish name, is densely spiked with the masts of grounded sailing ships from Boston and Baltimore, Sydney and Bremen, Hong Kong and Valparaiso. The muddy streets are thronged with Chinese in mushroom hats, Chileans in ponchos, Mississippi river rats with Bowie knives in their belts. The saloons, casinos and dance halls are jammed with miners uniformly dressed in red flannel shirts, knee boots, slouch hats and denim trousers caked with brick-red mud from the Mother Lode, the infinite vein of gold from which an amateur miner can scoop up a fortune in a frying pan. In our imagination we hear the honky-tonk piano at the El Dorado bar, the pistol shots, the midnight fire alarms and the tolling bell of the vigilance committee, bent upon administering swift and final judgment to murderous rogues from every part of the world. The neglected outpost of a faded empire has become the long-sought El Dorado, the mountain of gold.

The extravagant gold rush harbor of romantic myth lasted barely two years. The first wave of fortune hunters, who were bent on digging up a sack of glitter rock and heading home, was augmented—and, to some extent, actually *replaced*—by further waves of men and women looking for a new land where they could make their fortune in other ways —in buying and selling supplies, building houses,

MECHANICS' INSTITUTE
LIBRARY & CHESS ROOM

SINCE
1854

MECHANICS' INSTITUTE
57 POST STREET, STE. 504
SAN FRANCISCO, CA 94104

Place
Stamp
Here

MECHANICS'
INSTITUTE

SAN FRANCISCO IN 1854

running restaurants and hotels, opening bakeries, haberdasheries and furniture stores, publishing newspapers, preaching religion, starting families. Substantial structures of brick and stone replaced the wooden shacks and the hulls of sunken ships that briefly had served as stores along the waterfront. Protestants, Mormons, Unitarians and Jews established new congregations in the former territory of the old Franciscan mission. Clubs coagulated—Odd Fellows, Masons, marching societies, volunteer fire companies, an exclusive society of "California Pioneers," a German Turnverein. The city adopted a scheme of local government, based on the pattern of New York City. People began to talk about such ordinary matters as the high cost of imported food, tools and building materials; the lack of schools, libraries and cultural institutions; the dearth of local industries and paying jobs; the absence of comforting domestic life.

With its future still at hazard, San Francisco was beginning to feel the uncertainties, the disabilities of its irregular origin: its diverse, unskilled and unreliable population, its unbalanced economy, its isolation, its need of capital and industry. Most goods were imported, and there was no workforce of artisans, craftsmen and enterprising managers to build the future state.

As the historian Richard C. Wade has observed: "San Francisco's growth was neither inevitable nor tidy. Even its location was open to question and competition from the very beginning. In addition, after its regional supremacy was established, the young town suffered feasts and famine economically, continuous crime and outbursts of violence, and persistent poverty and deprivation. In addition, the speed of expansion made the planting of cultural roots precarious and the establishment of congenial social routines difficult."

Five years after the gold rush began, the easy gold was gone, and many disheartened Forty-Niners (those who had survived the ordeal) headed home. In the inevitable economic slump, several local banks failed and closed their doors. Although the banks had served primarily as agencies to gather and ship gold ingots out of California to parent companies in Europe and the eastern United States, their collapse exacerbated an existing shortage of capital and deepened the local economic depression.

Hopefully, almost wistfully, the town's most ardent boosters (Frank Soule, John H. Gihon and James Nisbet, in their 800-page *Annals of San Francisco*, published in 1855) hailed the construction of every new office building, theater, church or warehouse. Still, they admitted that the spectacular physical growth—in fact, the very existence—of the young city depended almost entirely on the production and exportation of gold. Against all odds, the writers of the *Annals* predicted that the prompt construction of a great "Atlantic and Pacific Railway" soon would bring agriculture, commerce, manufacturing and permanent prosperity to California.

It turned out that fourteen years would pass before the joining of the Central Pacific and Union Pacific railroads delivered those blessings to the West Coast. Meanwhile, in the rocky 1850s, the excitable, intensely ambitious and restlessly dissatisfied residents of San Francisco saw every downturn in gold production, every failed enterprise as a warning of the city's unstable economy and problematic future.

FIRST PEOPLE, COLONISTS AND GOLD RUSH PIONEERS

700 Ohlone Indian tribes, gathering plants and hunting animals in the tide flats and forests, live in scattered villages along the shores of the great bay.

1770 Spanish explorers sight San Francisco Bay for the first time.

1776 Spanish soldiers and priests establish a Presidio (military base) and a Catholic mission called San Francisco de Asis. A small, relatively unimportant port develops at Yerba Buena Cove.

1778 A Spanish census counts heads and finds 625 Indians and two priests at the Mission, plus 206 men and women, mostly soldiers and their wives, at the Presidio.

1822 Spanish rule ends in California as Mexico breaks away from Spain and designates "Alta California" a province of the Republic, with an appointed governor at Monterey.

1834 Mexican government grants pueblo status to Yerba Buena village and establishes local government headed by an appointed *alcalde*, who combines the roles of mayor, judge, party host and real estate developer.

1834–45 A series of nine Mexican *alcaldes* governs the pueblo, portioning out land to colonists according to the generous formula of the Mexican government.

1836 Juan Bautista Alvarado leads a radical reform movement that makes California an autonomous province.

1846 American colonists stage a bloodless revolution, raise a flag decorated with a grizzly bear over the Mexican army barracks in Sonoma and proclaim an independent republic that lasts one month (June 10–July 9).

THE FIRE OF MAY 4, 1851, viewed from Long Wharf.

SAMUEL WHITAKER AND ROBERT MCKENZIE were accused of robbery, convicted and hanged on cargo booms at the headquarters of the vigilantes on August 24, 1851.

1846 American troops occupy the pueblo of Yerba Buena in July and begin calling it San Francisco. The first American *alcalde*, a Navy lieutenant named Washington Allen Bartlett, takes civilian command and serves for about six months.

1847 Yerba Buena *officially* takes the name "San Francisco" to silence the claims of rivals such as Francisca (later Benicia) around the bay.

1848 James Marshall's discovery of gold on a January morning in the raceway of John Sutter's sawmill at Coloma, in the foothills of the Sierra Nevada, sets off the greatest gold rush in history.

1849 Gold hunters from every continent pour into California. The population of San Francisco explodes from around a thousand (1846) to about 50,000 highly impermanent newcomers.

1850 More than 600 vessels lie at anchor in San Francisco Bay ... California is admitted to the federal union as the thirty-first state ... John White Geary, elected *alcalde* under the Mexican system of government, becomes San Francisco's first mayor, American-style.

1851 Fires destroy almost the entire city (May) and, later, a portion of what is left (June) ... The first self-styled "Committee of Vigilance" hangs two men accused of burglary and drives other suspected criminals out of town.

1852 The *Golden Era*, San Francisco's premier literary weekly, edited by Rollin M. Daggett, first appears. Paying nothing for poetry and $5 per column for prose, the magazine becomes the platform for nearly every writer of prominence in California for the next decade ... Businessmen found the Mercantile Library at a meeting in City Hall.

1853 Shipments out of San Francisco (almost entirely gold bullion) peak at more than $57 million this year and begin a gradual decline ... Dr. Henry Durant founds a college—the future University of California—with three students and a $300-a-month operating budget in a former fandango house in Oakland.

1854 The San Francisco Branch of the United States Mint begins processing coins and blocks of bullion in a two-story building on Commercial Street. The first assayer is the enterprising Hungarian immigrant Agoston Haraszthy, better remembered for planting zinfandel grapes.

1854 In December, a small group of men in the building and manufacturing trades meets to establish the San Francisco Mechanics' Institute, a club-like library and community center for adult education, cultural and social activities.

A GREAT IDEA GETS A BAD START IN RISKY TIMES

THE YEAR 1854 was almost fatal for the little gold rush harbor on San Francisco Bay. The winter was the coldest anyone could remember. In January, piercing winds howled out of the north, and an inch of ice crunched in the ruts along the muddy streets. Water froze in pitchers overnight. To add to the misery, everyone seemed to have run out of money. The warehouses were glutted with unsold goods, imported in hope that the wildly profitable gold rush would last forever—or, at least, another year or two. Prices plunged, more banks failed, and an uncounted number of speculators gave up, declared bankruptcy or mysteriously disappeared. The ever-optimistic *Annals* admitted: "San Francisco is passing through a time of much mercantile distress."

In this dispiriting atmosphere, a group of workers in the construction trades met to consider a small but positive contribution they could make toward the survival of the beleaguered city. They would found an "institute"—a school of technology, a library and a lecture hall for the education and advancement of toilers in the field of "mechanical arts."

Like most social and cultural organizations established by the American conquerors of California, the Mechanics' Institute was a transplant from "back East." Similar institutes already were thriving and growing in Britain, Australia, Ireland and North America. Benjamin Franklin's "Library Company of Philadelphia" had been a successful stockholders' institution for more than ninety years. But who could be certain that an educational center for artisans would succeed in a small, new, very isolated commercial city, where the principal business activity was importing goods and commodities from other places, and virtually the only local product was gold?

The founders of the San Francisco Mechanics' Institute were neither social reformers nor educators, nor were they toilers from an oppressed underclass. Among the charter members were skilled machinists, carpenters, dealers in building supplies and manufacturers of such basic products as stoves, hand tools, wheels, barrels and wagons. Their common link was a boundless faith in the future of San Francisco as an industrial center—and an intense aversion to imported goods, which they believed kept

BEN FRANKLIN'S IDEA
A READING CLUB FOR MEN WITH MUCH AMBITION, LITTLE CASH

Twenty-one-year-old Benjamin Franklin, a job printer and sometime newspaper publisher in Philadelphia, organized a group of his fellow mechanics, inventors and free spirits into a debating club called The Junto, scornfully known to its wealthier detractors as "The Leathern Apron Club." Like the impoverished craftsmen of San Francisco more than a century later, the men of The Junto craved knowledge, economic power and political influence.

They needed reference books, standard works of history, philosophy and literature, the raw materials of higher education, which were then available only to prosperous book collectors. Franklin's practical answer was to pool the resources of the group and start a private library of their own.

In 1731, Franklin and his friends formed the Library Company of Philadelphia. Fifty subscribers put up forty shillings each for the purchase of books and agreed to pay ten shillings a year to maintain and grow the collection. Their motto, loosely translated from Latin, was "It is a divine act to share knowledge for the common good." The Library Company endures today on Locust Street, in the latest of its numerous homes, a treasury of Americana and a research center in American history.

GEORGE BIRKBECK'S SCHEME
THE SCOTTISH ORIGINS OF
THE "MECHANICS' INSTITUTE"

The inspiration for a "craftsmen's college," combining in one building an adult school, library and display of tools for men in the manufacturing and building trades, came from an English physician, George Birkbeck, who founded the first mechanics' institute, the Edinburgh School of Arts, in Scotland in 1821. Birkbeck had begun his energetic commitment to adult education several years earlier when he delivered a series of free lectures on modern technology to large crowds of unschooled workmen at a small technical university in Glasgow.

Birkbeck quit teaching and returned to his medical practice, but his continued interest in scientific education led him to carry his Scottish model to London, where he was able to raise money and support for a London Mechanics' Institute. The scheme was officially launched in November, 1823, at a public meeting said to have been attended by 2000 enthusiasts. By 1826 there were one hundred mechanics' institutes in Britain. By 1841 there were three hundred. Throughout the English-speaking world, in Canada, Australia, South Africa and the United States, the idea took hold of little groups of artisans who rented rooms, gathered books and started their own part-time colleges—the Franklin Institute of Philadelphia (1824), the Maryland Institute of Baltimore (1825), the Boston Mechanics' Institution (1827).

The London Institute survives as Birkbeck College of the University of London. The college calls itself Great Britain's "leading provider of face-to-face, part-time adult education." The curriculum includes business and computer studies and creative writing.

---

prices high and deprived local people of jobs and opportunities to develop their own businesses. Their stated and frequently demonstrated mission was to stimulate the growth of industry on the Pacific Coast, and they hoped to do this by igniting the ambitions and honing the practical skills of their fellow mechanics.

The founders held their first meeting on a winter night (December 11, 1854) in the tax collector's office at City Hall, one of the few gathering places in town without a religious, fraternal or fire-fighting function. Half a dozen men showed up. The presiding officer was George K. Guylas, a contract carpenter. The secretary was Roderick Matheson, a stone mason. Among the others were the owner of a sawmill, a blacksmith and a commission merchant. Having agreed to start an institute, they scattered to solicit donations, recruit members and draft a constitution with educational principles modeled on George Birkbeck's mechanics institute of London and a plan of subscription membership based on that of Benjamin Franklin's Library Company of Philadelphia.

By the next meeting (March 29, 1855) several of the first group had dropped out or been dropped. Five new officers and seven more or less permanent directors took over. The board was now headed by Benjamin Haywood, a substantial factory owner,

who had built one of the first sawmills in California up in the gold country. The vice president was John Sime, a building contractor; the treasurer, John W. Brooks, a prosperous manufacturer of stoves and hardware; the corresponding secretary, William LaRoche, a roaster and grinder of coffee; and the recording secretary, Peter Dexter, who was also the Institute's first librarian.

From the beginning, the directors knew what sort of library they wanted: Open stacks (or shelves) with access to all books by all members. A game room—or, to begin with, a secluded corner of the main room—where the members could spread out their chess and checker boards. Open hours from 10 to 10 daily, except Sundays, Christmas Day, New Year's Day and the Fourth of July. To finance the venture, they would offer shares of stock at $25, with $3 dues per quarter, or non-voting subscriptions at $5, with the same dues. As they saw it, this plan would result in an Institute with 3000 voting members and $75,000 in capital.

In those bleak days, however, the $5 initiation fee and the $12 yearly dues struck many San Franciscans as insurmountably high. As for stock ownership at $25—that was perhaps equivalent to $500 in current values. At the end of the first year, there were only two hundred stockholders and few non-voting members.

THE INSTITUTE FINDS *(and outgrows)* ITS FIRST HOME, FINDS *(and dislikes)* ITS SECOND

JUST SIX MONTHS after their first, small gathering at City Hall, the founders of the Institute located and rented quarters for their library—a single, top-floor room in the most conspicuous new structure in San Francisco, the four-story Express Building at the northeast corner of California and Montgomery Streets. The "library" consisted of one two-volume study of architecture and three essential reference works—the United States Constitution, the Bible and a law text on the conveyance of property. The Chess Club occupied a corner. The treasury totaled $300, out of which the librarian, a dedicated board member named Peter B. Dexter, had to blow two whole dollars on candles to avoid the costly alternative, gaslight.

Years later, Andrew S. Hallidie, the most creative and influential president in the long history of the Institute, admitted to an audience of librarians: "On the whole, but little headway was made during the first year." After four months, the book collection had grown to only 75 volumes. The treasury was down to $125. By the end of the year, the library possessed 487 volumes and roughly $21 in cash. Among the donations had been a volume of sermons from an unidentified benefactor, whose gift, according to

Hallidie, put a crimp in the library's efforts to recruit members. The librarian's expenditure for candles in lieu of gas had mounted to $13.

A few months into its second year, the Institute faced another financial crisis. No sooner had the librarian moved the books, chess boards, cuspidors and potted palms out of the fourth-floor room on Montgomery Street into larger quarters at 110 California Street than he reported that, once again, he was fresh out of money. To make things worse, the new place was dark and out of the way, and even more expensive ($65 a month) than the Express Building. It was so unpopular that no one bothered to draw its picture or add a photograph of it to the archives. Mr. Dexter, who had no other employment, offered to stay on the job without salary while the directors cast about for cash.

WHEN IT OPENED in January, 1854, the Express Building—named for the Wells Fargo Bank and Express Company on the street floor—was the most stately structure on Montgomery Street: a four-story, $180,000 building on a lot valued at $100,000. The ever-enthusiastic writers of the *Annals of San Francisco* hailed it as "another of Mr. Samuel Brannan's magnificent street improvements." Mr. Brannan, a land speculator, vigilante organizer and defrocked elder of the Church of Latter-Day Saints, was an immigrant to California in 1846. He is credited with setting off the stampede to the Sierra in 1848 by walking the streets, showing off a sample of glitter from Sutter's Mill. That the Mechanics' Institute could rent a fourth-floor room for only $25 attested to the generosity of Mr. Brannan—or perhaps a shortage of tenants. The other upstairs occupants were a brokerage called Pollard & Co. and the Society of California Pioneers. The Society, like the Mechanics' Institute, has survived a century and a half of unstable subsoil and changing locations.

SAM BUGBEE'S GIFT

Like most San Franciscans in 1855, Samuel Charles Bugbee was a newcomer, fresh off the boat from Boston. Unlike most others, Bugbee was a trained professional, a practicing architect. At the ripe age of forty-three, he had behind him two decades of experience designing buildings in New England. To the little group of carpenters, black- smiths, plumbers and contractors who were trying to organize a Mechanics' Institute in a raw new city, far from traditional sources of publica- tion and inspiration, Sam Bugbee was a welcome advisor. He attended their first meetings and served for a few months as a member of the board of directors. More important, he offered to supply the Institute with its first books.

Bugbee's choices—probably from his own library—reflected not only his own commit- ment to essential works but also his sense of the practical purposes of a technical library in a setting that offered no opportunities for adult education. His selections were the Bible; the United States Constitution; George Tichnor Curtis's *American Conveyances* (a standard legal reference since its first publication in 1833); and the immense, two-volume *Encyclopaedia of Cottage, Farm and Villa Architecture*, published a few years earlier by Britain's leading authorities on landscape gardening, the Scottish-born John C. Loudon and his wife, Jane Webb Loudon.

STATELY MANSIONS Bugbee became one of the city's leading architects in the decades of the 1860s and '70s. He designed the Nob Hill mansions of Leland Stanford, Richard Tobin, David Colton and Mark Hopkins, and the most imposing theater in western America, the 1600-seat California Theatre at 444 Bush Street. He adapted the design of the renowned glass house in London's Kew Gardens to a glass conservatory for the estate of James Lick, a significant benefactor of the Mechanics' Institute. After Lick's death, the Conservatory was purchased by a group of philanthropic San Franciscans who had it moved and installed in Golden Gate Park. Most of Bugbee's domestic architecture disappeared in (or even before) the earthquake and fire of 1906. The California Theatre, "guaranteed" by Bugbee to withstand both earthquake and fire, also succumbed. The Conservatory alone remains, delighting millions with its ferns, orchids and giant water lilies.

LOST GAINS As for Sam Bugbee's gift to the Mechanics', someone made off almost immediately with the Bible and the U.S. Constitution, reducing the number of vol- umes in the library by half. For the Mechanics', this was the first recorded instance of the sort of pilferage that plagues libraries the world over. Soon, however, the library was blessed with two volumes donated by one H. A. Miller (who probably was *not* the German-born butcher who later became California's largest landowner and uncrowned "Cattle King"). Next came thirty-nine volumes of U.S. government documents, given by Representative James A. McDougall, a former state attorney general and future U.S. senator. The directors of the Mechanics', in gratitude to Congressman McDougall, hung his lithographed portrait in a gilt-edged frame in the Institute's first reading room. Sam Bugbee was not so honored, but in remembrance of his gift, equivalent editions of the five original volumes were restored to the library in celebration of the Institute's hundred-and-fiftieth anniversary in 2004–5.

TURMOIL IN THE CITY, A SLOW YEAR AT THE LIBRARY

THE HISTORIAN David Lavender in *Nothing Seemed Impossible*, a biography of San Francisco's historic entrepreneur William C. Ralston, wrote:

> *Believing in San Francisco's future during the dreadful year of 1856 took an act of supreme faith. The financial downswing, born of the excesses of the early 1850s and intensified by the bank failures of 1855, showed no sign of ending.*

In mid-May of that "dreadful year," the murder of a vitriolic newspaper editor, James King of William, by a city councilman, James Casey, whom King had libeled, stirred up a civil insurrection that has been called the "Business Men's Revolution." For the next four months the streets trembled to

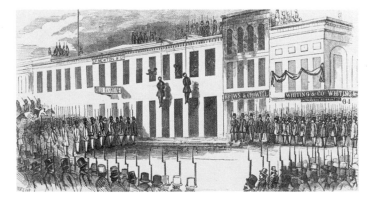

THE HANGING OF CHARLES CORA AND JAMES CASEY from the pediment of "Fort Gunnybags" at 41 Sacramento Street. Some San Franciscans, then as now, saw the "vigilance" as an unjustified descent into violence in contempt of law, an indelible blot on the reputation of the city; to others, it appeared to be a justified revolution, a triumph of civic rectitude over the corruption of an evil political regime.

the footsteps of marching riflemen and the tolling bell at "Fort Gunnybags," the headquarters of the revolutionary committee on Sacramento Street near the waterfront.

Before the "Committee of Vigilance" had completed its self-appointed task of purging and replacing the city's political leaders (who the vigilantes maintained had been elected by fraud), four accused criminals (including the assassin of James King of William) had been hanged on a newly built gallows outside Fort Gunnybags; numerous other alleged miscreants had been formally exiled out of the Golden Gate, and uncounted numbers had been persuaded by the threat of prosecution to leave the city. More than 7000 men had signed the secret roster as members of the "Committee."

No one could have ignored the vigilance, and few were able to avoid taking sides in the ensuing political purge, but there is no evidence that the Mechanics' Institute played an active role for or against the vigilance. Carpenters, iron smiths, painters and carriage makers were among the thousands of vigilantes, but the leadership was clearly of the merchant class, the get-rich-quick traders, the bankers and lawyers whose interests, for the most part, were opposed by the mechanics.

On the afternoon of May 14, the day James Casey shot and mortally wounded James King of William, the directors of the Mechanics' Institute had been holding a regular meeting, presumably to discuss and bemoan their chronic shortage of cash and their continued lack of success in recruiting new members. Although the library had grown to 500 volumes, the Institute was still in debt and losing money. Apparently, the directors ended their talk and recessed that afternoon before learning that King had been shot and carried, fatally wounded, into the Bank Exchange Saloon, where volunteer doctors were trying to stanch his bleeding with an unsterilized sponge. The next two meetings of the directors, on May 20 and 27, were recessed for lack of a quorum.

It was during the height of the vigilantes' control of the city that a savior appeared for the Mechanics'—an actress from the outside world, who gave the Institute another year of life.

AN ACTRESS SAVES THE FALTERING LIBRARY WITH A BENEFIT PERFORMANCE

Julia Dean Hayne, the toast of Charleston, had scarcely arrived in San Francisco in May, 1856, when she was enlisted to rescue the fledgling Mechanics' Institute. A year after opening its one-room library and chess room, the Institute was flat broke. A hundred and fifty years later, no one seems to know or care whether Miss Hayne had ever heard of the Institute, knew any of its founders or subscribed to its goals—or whether she was merely seeking the attention of a new audience. In any case, she agreed—or volunteered—to do a special performance of her current dramatic vehicle, *Madeleine, the Belle of Faubourg,* on a July evening in 1856 at the Metropolitan Theatre, with the net proceeds going to the struggling little library.

THE METROPOLITAN THEATRE, an "elegant temple of histrionic art" on Montgomery Street between Washington and Jackson, opened on Christmas Eve, 1854. It was neither the largest nor grandest theater in town, but it boasted being one of the safest: it was built of brick in a town where wooden buildings had a notorious tendency to burn down. The Metropolitan did not burn down until August 14, 1857.

Miss Hayne, who had just turned twenty-six, had come to San Francisco as a mature and widely recognized performer. Born into the life of the theater, she was the daughter of an actress and a theatrical manager in upstate New York, and she had made her first appearance on stage at age fifteen. By sixteen, she had won and thereafter virtually owned the leading role—that of a woman named Julia—in a play called *The Hunchback.* After touring New York, Philadelphia and other cities, she had taken *The Hunchback* to Charleston, South Carolina. In a sense, Julia Hayne still resides in Charleston, dressed for her famous role in *The Hunchback,* in a mural of the twenty-five leading personalities in Charleston's two-hundred-year theatrical history. The historic notes of Charleston's "Footlight Players" record that "so great was her charm that a group of local admirers presented her with a specially designed bracelet and breast-pin set with emeralds, diamonds and pearls." Among her ardent admirers was one Dr. Arthur Hayne, whom she married and with whom she came to San Francisco, in the nick of time to save the Mechanics' Institute from bankruptcy.

Mrs. Julia Dean Haynes as Juliet.

AN ENDURING GIFT The Metropolitan Theatre and *Madeleine, the Belle of Faubourg* have joined the dust of forgotten entertainments, but Julia Hayne's donation has endured. The $1029 that she earned at the benefit performance, along with a few new memberships at $1 a year, kept the Institute alive for another twelve months, when, of necessity, the directors began to scratch around for new revenue.

Julia Hayne moved on from San Francisco, shed Dr. Hayne on grounds of non-support, remarried, played many roles (comedy and juvenile tragedy were her forte) and died at age thirty-seven, still beautiful, still seeking new stages for *The Hunchback* and for Madeleine, Juliet and her other beloved roles.

THE MECHANICS BUILD A PALACE
FOR THE CITY'S INFANT INDUSTRIES

AT THE BEGINNING of its third year, 1857, the Mechanics' Institute again faced collapse. The supply of easy gold that had sustained the fragile economy of California was running down. The little boomtown of San Francisco was shrinking almost visibly as disappointed fortune hunters packed up and drifted away. The humble Mechanics' Institute, with its 900-volume library, its quiet chess room and its lofty plans to bring higher education to workers in metal, wood and stone, now attracted few members at $6 a year, and even fewer stockholders at $25 a share. The directors reduced the quarterly dues from $3 to $1.50, but membership still lagged. There was little hope that another actress like Julia Hayne might again save the Institute from bankruptcy.

With the encouragement of several prosperous businessmen, including James Lick, Samuel Brannan and Thomas O. Larkin, the directors—most of whom were workmen in the building trades—fixed on a grandiose project to lift the Institute out of its chronic poverty and stir the city out of its economic stagnation. They would design and build with their own hands an exposition—a local version of the great international expositions that had invigorated London in 1851 and New York City in 1853. They would call their show *The First Industrial Exhibition of the Mechanics' Institute of the City of San Francisco.*

The grandeur of their ambition was revealed in their first announcement to the public.

"Fairs," they said, "besides exciting emulation, extending practical knowledge, suggesting ideas to ingenious minds, affording tangible evidence of superiority, stimulating talent, exhibiting the progress of the city, promoting extensive intercourse among producers and their patrons [etc.] cannot fail to excite a world-wide interest in regard to our State, and extend reliable information respecting its resources, which will tend to encourage immigration and permanently establish beneath our genial skies an industrious, enlightened, prosperous and happy population."

A FESTIVE PAVILION WITH MOORISH MINARETS and fluttering banners housed the First Mechanics' Industrial Fair (September 7–28, 1857) on the west side of Montgomery Street between Post and Sutter Streets.

ABOVE LEFT *New York's Crystal Palace, 1853.* The first industrial exhibition in the United States took its name, its style, and its claim to glory from London's Crystal Palace Exposition of 1851. The sponsors were some of the richest men in New York, but even they could not afford to reproduce the original Crystal Palace. They passed over Joseph Paxton, the inspired horticulturist who had based the dome of his masterpiece on the leaf ribs of the *Victoria regia* water lily, in favor of the Danish architect George Carstensen, chief designer of the Tivoli Gardens in Copenhagen. Carstensen collaborated with an American, Charles Guildmeister, in drawing up plans for an immense octagonal box with a dome of painted wood. Although it offered only one-fifth the exhibit space of the great hall in London, it was much the finest pleasure dome that anyone had seen on this side of the Atlantic. The poet Walt Whitman was awestruck. Years later, he recalled, "A Palace / Loftier, fairer, ampler than any yet."

ABOVE RIGHT *San Francisco's Canvas Cousin, 1857.* The Mechanics' Institute enlisted two of its own members to design and build (at minimum cost and maximum speed) a magnificent showplace for the products and artistry of California. Reuben Clark, a carpenter from Maine, and German-born Henry Kenitzer, who would later become a partner of the more famous San Francisco architect David Farquharson, took on the job. Clark, who had once worked on the state capitol of Mississippi, later designed and supervised one of several early and unfinished capitol buildings in Sacramento—as did Kenitzer. Although their talents were unknown and untried in California, they apparently were familiar with the outward appearance of New York's Crystal Palace and knew exactly how an industrial exposition ought to look—even a very small, three-week industrial exposition in a very small, very isolated city.

That no single event could have achieved such results apparently did not dishearten the leaders of the Institute. Nor were they put off by the fact (if they knew it) that New York's Crystal Palace Exposition had lost more than $300,000 of its stockholders' investment. Nor that their projected exposition building, at 20,000 square feet, would be one-tenth the size of the exhibition in New York (which in turn was only one-fifth the size of London's Crystal Palace). Nor that the San Francisco exhibition would last only three weeks. Nor that the Institute momentarily possessed roughly $300 in cash.

James Lick, the city's protomillionaire, who earlier had donated rent-free space for the Mechanics' first library, offered the free use of a lot he owned on the west side of Montgomery Street between Post and Sutter Streets, way out on the southwest edge of town. The leaders and members of the Institute raised $7000 in cash, materials and short-term loans and went to work.

The exhibition netted $2784.48 in cash to the Institute, plus the building, valued at $3500, which was sturdy enough to use for occasional meetings and for another fair the next year. The Institute gave $626 of the proceeds to the Protestant orphanage and an equal sum to the Catholic orphanage and invested $1000 of the remainder in books for the library.

More important, perhaps, was that the exposition showed the products of California's infant economy and raised a cry for more industrial development. At the opening ceremonies, Henry F. Williams, a building contractor and charter member, railed against what he called "a system of excessive importations" that was impoverishing the region by pouring out millions in gold in return for "useless articles."

"We will wage a war against the importers who are still draining us of all the gold obtained from the mines," Williams declared. He insisted that California's mineral wealth must be used to purchase products made "at home." Williams's call to "buy local" must have rung pleasantly in the ears of the coopers and furniture makers, saddlers, iron wrights, quilters and cobblers who were displaying their wares in the little canvas-domed pavilion on Montgomery Street.

WHAT THEY SAW
WHAT THEY SHOWED
WHAT THEY SANG

Great works of art were there to view,
And mechanisms rare,
There Genius proudly reigned supreme
At the "Exhibition Fair"!

THE UNCROWNED LAUREATE of the First Mechanics' Fair was Edward Pollock, a local wordsmith, most of whose other verses have been lost to posterity. At the opening ceremonies on September 7, 1857, Mr. Pollock declaimed an ode several hundred lines long, beginning:

Mechanics! To your hands we owe
Whatever we behold below,
From nature taken, and designed
To suit the changing human mind.

Afterward, Mr. S. A. Wells, one of the city's reigning baritones, sang a rousing anthem called "The Exhibition Fair," composed by Mr. P. R. Nicholls, which opens:

Yes! Proud may be the Institute
That reared the mighty scheme.
And California hence shall be
The poets' happy theme.

THE BEST ENTRIES IN EACH CATEGORY were awarded silver or bronze medals, designed by the celebrated artist Charles Nahl, and diplomas of merit, also designed by Nahl and printed by Britton and Rey, the premier lithographers in town. Nowadays, the medals and certificates of the thirty-one Mechanics' Fairs, like the paintings of Charles Nahl, are found in museums and historical archives. In their day, they honored such products as Larkin's Carriages, Denniston's Silver-Plated Amalgamating Plates, and Levi Strauss's copper-riveted denim trousers.

The aforementioned "great works of art" and "mechanisms rare" were divided into forty-five classes, including one for miscellaneous entries such as smoked beef, cigars, a lamp that burned lard, some silkworms, an assortment of imitation asphalt roofing materials, and so on. There were separate divisions for furniture; rope; onyx; building stone and granite; saddles and harnesses; billiard tables; pianos; barrels; shoes; and buggies.

Among the great works by busy hands at home were embroidery, needle, wax, shell, and hair work. There were coverlets made of quilting, crocheted yarn and raccoon skin; an assortment of palm-leaf baskets; and a jar of quince jelly. George Yount, the pioneer rancher of Napa Valley, submitted a sack of flour from his "Star of the West" mill. Yount's neighbor, J. W. Osborne of Oak Knoll Farm, exhibited wine grapes grown from imported stock, including a little-known variety called "*Zinfindal*." A British-born printers' agent named E. J. Muygridge (later and better known as Eadweard Muybridge) showed a set of his lithographs. Along the aisles of the pavilion one also could see (among the nine hundred listed entries) a lump of coal from Coos Bay, Oregon; bits of petrified wood, sulfur, borax, copper ore and silver ore; an autographed letter from the New England despot Cotton Mather; and a glass jar containing a horned toad.

Significantly, there were major displays of the local industrial products that the Mechanics' Institute hoped to encourage with its educational programs: iron railings from the Eureka Key & Clamp Works owned by William McKibbin, one of the founders of the Institute; sugar from the recently established San Francisco Sugar Refinery; bars of chocolate made by Domenico Ghirardelli; a steam engine from the Vulcan Iron Company, headed by another Mechanics' founder, Daniel Van Pelt; and samples of polished brass and water pumps from Thomas H. Selby, a founder of the Mercantile Association, who later would establish the largest ore smelter in California, with one of the tallest smokestacks in the world.

A RICH RIVAL
WITH A
HEAD START

SAN FRANCISCO'S MERCANTILE LIBRARY, like the Mechanics' Institute, was modeled on an East Coast prototype—in this case, the Mercantile Library of New York—which, in turn, was inspired by Franklin's Library Company of Philadelphia. Two years before the organization of the Mechanics' Institute, the founders of the Mercantile, including many of the leading businessmen in town, held an enthusiastic, well-attended meeting (December 22, 1852) at City Hall. On the spot, they enlisted $6000 in pledges. Less than two months later, they had rented rooms in a convenient building at the center of town, opened their reading room to members and elected a nine-man slate of officers headed by David S. Turner, a wholesale auctioneer.

Turner was an appropriate representative of the gold-rush merchants of San Francisco, most of whom made their living by selling food, clothing, furniture and building materials—almost anything that could be imported by ship, ox cart or donkey-back—at enormous profit (or, when the market was glutted, using the surplus cargo to pave a street or dumping it in the tidal mud along the bay). In a sense, the merchants who founded the Mercantile Association were the economic rivals, the class enemies of the would-be manufacturers who started the Mechanics' Institute two years later.

The core of the Mercantile Library was a 2500-volume collection purchased from Brigadier General Ethan Allen Hitchcock, a grandson of Ethan Allen, the Vermont revolutionary patriot. General Hitchcock was en route back east after completing a command in Mexico City, and he was willing to part with his vast personal library, rich in works on alchemy, religion and the philosophy of Swedenborg, Spinoza and Jesus. The gravity of General Hitchcock's collection guaranteed the Mercantile a position as the city's premier cultural institution.

Among the rules of conduct at the dignified Mercantile: "No member will be allowed to remain in the Library or Reading Room with his hat on.... The Reading Room may be occupied exclusively by ladies and gentlemen accompanying ladies, between the hours of 12 and 2 P.M."

The first public program, two weeks after a well-publicized and fatal duel, was a debate on the timely question "Is Dueling Justified Under Any Circumstances?" It is not recorded which argument prevailed.

By the end of the year, the Mercantile Association reported that it was free of debt, owned 4000 books, countless newspapers and innumerable magazines, and had on hand several hundred dollars in cash. The monthly expenses were running $200 for rent, $175 for librarian, $80 for assistant librarian, and $145 for "incidentals." With 472 members, each paying $1 a month, the Mercantile was not meeting its expenses but hoped to do so by attracting more shareholders at $25.

Twelve months later, after another successful year, Board President Turner admitted that membership in the Mercantile was still limited mainly to merchants and the clerks of merchants, but he was pleased to note that "the mechanics of our city" had met to create a rival institution "for their own class."

"We hail with pleasure the efforts to organize and establish the Mechanics' Association, and bid them 'God speed,'" Turner said.

In truth, it was the beginning of a half-century of competition for members, prestige and financial survival between the two subscription libraries in one small, insecure and economically unstable city. The Mercantile began in strength, and for several years it seemed destined to outgrow and surpass its rival. In its ninth year of operation (1859), the president boasted that it was "the principal [library] on the Pacific Coast, and probably will long continue to be so."

The membership, he said, was no longer confined to merchants and their clerks but included also "mechanics, men of leisure, and members of all learned professions." The most popular category of books (Romance and Fiction) had circulated 3626 volumes in the previous year, whereas the least popular (Law, Politics and Jurisprudence) had circulated 95. President Henry M. Hale concluded: "I am happy to say that I do not know of an objectionable book in the library, judged by the ordinary moral standards."

GOLD AND SILVER
AND DISTANT WAR

1857   The total value of exports from San Francisco (mostly gold) since the first departure of a steamer for Panama in April, 1849, is now close to $375 million—a significant lump in the national economy—but the amount per year is falling.

1858   In February, a sample of gold from the Fraser River, British Columbia, reaches the San Francisco Mint on a Hudson's Bay Company ship, and the news sets off a new gold rush. Within the year, 30,000 men—many of them from San Francisco—are staking claims in western Canada. The sudden loss of population sends San Francisco into its worst economic slump since 1850. One result: The Mechanics' Second Industrial Fair that September nets only $772. The pavilion is scrapped and the materials are sold for $1200.

1859   (July) First news from Nevada of rich gold and silver discoveries in Washoe County and on the Truckee River ... (September 13) The machinery

THE MERCANTILE ASSOCIATION opened its first reading and meeting room in the California Exchange Building at the corner of Clay and Kearny Streets on Portsmouth Square, the historic plaza at the heart of the city, on February 1, 1853.

for the U.S. steamer *Saginaw* is completed at the Union Iron Foundry, first work of the kind in California ... (September 16) David C. Broderick, junior United States senator from California, is fatally shot in a pistol duel with David S. Terry, Chief Justice of the California Supreme Court ... (September 18) Col. E. D. Baker delivers a moving eulogy over Broderick's coffin in the plaza, in which he charges that pro-slavery rivals marked Broderick for death because of his stand for abolition and against the corruption of the Buchanan administration.

1860   The first pony express reaches San Francisco (April 14) from St. Joseph, Missouri ... Service begins on the city's first street railway, from lower Market Street to Mission Dolores ... The town's favorite boulevardier, Joshua A. Norton, having previously declared himself Norton I, Emperor of the United States, gives orders to dissolve the United States.

1860   The mines of Nevada's Comstock Lode create the fortunes of many San Franciscans, notably the four Irish-born "Silver Kings" (the quartz mine owner James G. Fair; the pick-handling digger John W. Mackay; and the saloon keepers James C. Flood and William S. O'Brien) as well as the German-born mining engineer Adolph Sutro, the Missouri-born prospector George Hearst, the English-born politician John P. Jones (Nevada's "Silver Republican" U.S. senator for thirty years); and the bankers William Sharon and William Ralston.

1861   A mass meeting of working men convenes (August 1) at Mechanics' Hall to form a "Mechanics' League" to oppose the increasing use of convict labor in California. After several more meetings, the Mechanics' League joins the Anti-Coolie Association in a campaign for legislation "to protect [white, free-born] workers against [the competition of] convict and Chinese labor."

THE THIRD FAIR

Inspirited by the success of their first two expositions, the Mechanics' decreed another stately dome on James Lick's lot at Sutter and Montgomery Streets. A forty-man crew built the one-story wooden hall, based on a simple plan by three directors of the Institute—John E. Kincaid, Gardner Elliott, and Benjamin Dore—in two weeks. There was no dome. By July the Pavilion, advertised as "one of the largest Halls in the world," was in frequent use: for Independence Day tableaux and oratory, for a Grand Promenade Concert and Festival, and for a New England–style feast of pork and beans, pumpkin pies, buckwheat cakes, doughnuts and cheese to benefit the Deaf, Dumb and Blind. The Institute announced a fifteen-day Third Industrial Exposition to begin September 3.

The festivities commenced off-site with an address at the recently opened Platt's Musical Hall by Vice President J. W. Cherry, a house and sign painter by trade. Cherry's speech was "occasionally applauded and was listened to with much attention," according to next morning's *Alta California*, but the turnout was ominously thin. Thousands of men had left the city that year to stake claims for silver and gold in Nevada. Without these patrons, the fair was a fiasco. The directors of the Institute were so chagrined that they never published a report on their crippling financial loss. Members and friends intervened to rescue the library with donations and programs, but there would be no more industrial fairs for several years.

A few weeks after the fair closed, Abraham Lincoln was elected president. The news, brought by the Pony Express with unprecedented speed, did not reach San Francisco until November 15. Thousands of San Franciscans reacted with fireworks and torchlight parades. On November 23, the Pony Express brought word that Alabama and South Carolina had seceded from the federal union. Less than five months later, the Civil War began (April 12, 1861) with the Confederate attack on the Union army at Fort Sumter, South Carolina.

1862 Technically neutral, California supports the Union cause in the Civil War and supplies gold to Lincoln's army. The "California Hundred," a volunteer cavalry company, leaves San Francisco for the East Coast via Panama.

1863 Construction of the Central Pacific, the western portion of the great transcontinental railroad, begins in Sacramento, headed east.

1863 Rejuvenated by new members and successful public lectures, the Mechanics' Institute borrows $8500, buys a site at 529 California Street between Montgomery and Kearny Streets, constructs a building and moves its Chess Room and its library— now 5000 volumes and growing—to new quarters.

1863 The Institute sponsors a public forum in which business and political leaders urge the state legislature to retain California's unique money system—the free circulation of gold— against federal efforts to force the use of paper currency, anathema to San Francisco's dedicated metalists ... A group of businessmen, headed by the aggressive financier William C. Ralston, founder and president of the Bank of California, raises $2500 to pay off the Institute's second mortgage.

1864 Dr. H. H. Toland founds a small medical and surgical college on Stockton Street. Taken over by the State of California in 1872, the college becomes a school of the University of California in 1902. Greatly expanded and diversified during the next century, the University of California at San Francisco grows into a world center of medical training, patient treatment and scientific research.

THE FOURTH FAIR

In the midst of war, a welcome revival of San Francisco's most peaceful diversion

To HOUSE the fourth of its increasingly popular industrial fairs, the Institute risked $10,000 to build a grandiose temporary pavilion on a sandy, city-owned lot at the southwest corner of Geary and Stockton Streets, a derelict location on the outermost edge of the downtown district. It was the first such event since the outbreak of the Civil War, and the city obviously hoped it would encourage other building around the new plaza that had been named, in the spirit of the times, "Union Square."

Designed by P. J. O'Connor, a British-born architect who had recently become a director of the Institute, the new pavilion was a lighthearted, vaguely Baroque confection, spiky with towers and flag-poles and skinny buttresses. Its cruciform layout, its hundred-foot dome, its massive pediment and its twin towers all bore a strong family resemblance to the first Mechanics' pavilion of 1857 and its antecedents, the Crystal Palaces of London and New York. The main hall was a one-story wooden shed, as homely as a warehouse. Fingers of daylight poked through the cracks in its thin redwood siding. But the tacky structure enclosed 55,000 square feet of exhibit space—ample room for a miniature skating pond, a hedge labyrinth, a 40-foot tower of flowers, and the West's greatest display of quartz crushers and

THE THIRD PAVILION, at Geary and Stockton, echoed the first.

grindstones, loaves of sugar, mounds of apples, carrots and pears, piles of cowhide, bundles of wool, pinnacles of bottled vegetables and patented cordials such as Ladies' Tear Punch and The Soul's Consolation Syrup—and what next? The side galleries were given over to a display of paintings, photographs and sculpture, a restaurant and a music hall. With the exhibits out, the pavilion could seat 8000 for a concert, with standing room for 7000 more.

When all the exhibits were in place, the most notable landscape and stereographic photographer on the Pacific Coast, Carleton E. Watkins, positioned his cameras in the empty hall and began taking a series of his stereopticon views that later won a medal at the international exposition in Paris.

The purpose of the fair, as stated in the gassy language of the opening ceremonies, was not simply to entertain. It was:

To foster the Mechanic Arts, elevate the character of the workman, and stimulate ingenuity, invention, skill and industry in all their branches, in the hope of exercising a wholesome influence upon the general prosperity of the country.

Allowing that no exposition could or ever did attain such goals, the fair was a popular and financial success. For a full month, crowds of men and women and children wandered the great hall (though never on Sundays, of course). The newspapers reported on the exhibition every day, whether or not there was anything to say. First, they covered the fireworks, blazing in the sky at Geary and Stockton Streets, the speeches, and the singing; then the first impressions—curiosity, confusion, amazement; and, after that, the exhibits, one by one; the visitors lining up to see the giant cheese, the minor incidents and accidents; until, at last, the final burst of pyrotechnics and oratory blew the show away, leaving the vacant pavilion for eager customers to rent and use for costume balls, cello recitals and cautionary sermons.

Out of its risky venture, the Institute gained not only a huge new pavilion for future use, but also more than $3400 to run its library, chess room and classes. After the last bills had been paid, the trustees donated $1368 to help impoverished farmers in Santa Barbara County, one of the areas of the state severely crippled by a winter drought that had virtually destroyed the cattle industry.

THE FLORAL FOUNTAIN, a 40-foot latticework pyramid overgrown with vines and flowers, stood at the center of the Mechanics' Institute's new pavilion at the edge of Union Square. Around the base of the six-tiered ziggurat, jets of water splashed into a pool ringed with marble statues. Visitors who contributed 25 cents to the Sanitary Commission—the Civil War precursor to the American Red Cross—could cross a bridge, walk inside and see for themselves the unique treasures of the fair—a brick of Nevada silver worth $4200 from the Gould & Curry mine in Virginia City; and a 3936-pound cheese, locally made by T. S. Neagle's dairy and held in shape with a steel hoop, made and donated to the cause by Steele Brothers foundry of Santa Cruz. The hoop, which weighed almost as much as the cheese, could be unclamped while the cheese was turned and scraped. It competed for top honors in Class XXXVI—Domestic Machinery—with washing machines, sewing machines, wringers and churns. After the fair, the display traveled eastward, picking up further contributions to the Sanitary Commission. It wound up in New York City, where they chopped up the cheese and sold it at $1 a pound.

SAM CLEMENS
(aka Mark Twain)
GOES TO THE FAIR AND LIKES WHAT HE SEES

AMONG THOSE PRESENT was none other than Sam Clemens of Hannibal, Missouri, working nowadays under the pen name "Mark Twain." After several years in the mining country of Nevada, writing burlesques, hoaxes and satirical news articles for various magazines and newspapers (especially the *Territorial Enterprise* in the boom town of Virginia City), Sam had come down to San Francisco in May, 1864, hoping to ride high on the fruits of a speculation in mining stock. When the stock tanked, he was forced to take a job instead at the *San Francisco Call*, writing virtually every word in the newspaper. Among his less exhausting tasks was a daily report from the Mechanics' Fair. On the day before the Fair opened, he wrote:

The stern, practical appearance which the great array of machinery and all manner of industrial implements has heretofore given to the Pavilion is being softened and relieved, now, by a pleasant sprinkling of fresh flowers and beautiful pictures; and by the time the Art halls are fully dressed with paintings, and the central tower with blooming plants, and the fountain below filled with limpid water, and the thousand lights a-blaze above a mass of people in ceaseless motion, the place will be as vivacious and charming as it now looks tumbled and shapeless.

Twain was fired by the *Call* after four months of writing this sort of twaddle. He found a less demanding outlet for his work at the literary weekly *Golden Era*, edited by his friend Bret Harte, and at the *Californian*, a weekly that paid by the word. In the *Californian* he reported:

[The Pavilion] is a nice place to hunt for people in. I have hunted for a friend there for as much as two hours of an evening, and at the end of that time found the hunting just as good as it was when I commenced. . . .

I cannot say that all visitors to the Fair go there to make love, though I have my suspicions that a good many of them do. Numbers go there to look at the machinery and misunderstand it, and still greater numbers, perhaps, go to criticize the pictures. There is a handsome portrait in the Art Gallery of a pensive young girl. Last night it fell under the critical eye of a connoisseur from Arkansas. She examined it in silence for many minutes, and then she blew her nose calmly, and, says she, "I like it—it is so sad and thinkful."

ALONG THE AISLE leading to the six-tiered Flower Pyramid and its giant cheese was the glistening white "sugar selection" of the San Francisco and Pacific Refining Company, which won a top award for its sugars "refined, loaf, crystallized, crushed and powdered." Piled up like the peaks of Rio de Janeiro, the sugars were protected from "flies, gnats and touchy fingers" by a tent of white mosquito netting. A few steps along is the mysterious "electric clock," said to be run by a "regulator" on Montgomery Street, more than four blocks away.

THE MORE-OR-LESS TRUE
STORY OF A BUSTED BUST

AS REPORTED BY MARK TWAIN IN
THE CALIFORNIAN, OCTOBER 1, 1864

Somebody knocked Weller's bust down from its shelf at the Fair the other night, and destroyed it.

[That would be John B. Weller, a former U.S. senator and governor of California (1858–60). Weller, a pro-slavery Democrat, had been appointed Minister to Mexico by the lame-duck President Buchanan in 1860, and then quickly recalled by Lincoln because of his Southern sympathies. Here, at the Mechanics' Fair, he was immortalized in the robe of a Roman senator, a style of dress not approved in California for Confederate politicians.]

It was wrong to do it, but it gave rise to a very able pun by a young person who has had much experience in such things, and was only indifferently proud of it. He said it was Weller enough when it was a bust, but just the reverse when it was busted. Explanation: He meant that it looked like Weller in the first place, but it did not after it was smashed to pieces. He also meant that it was well enough to leave it alone and not destroy it. The Author of this fine joke is among us yet, and I can bring him around if you would like to look at him. One would expect him to be haughty and ostentatious, but you would be surprised to see how simple and unpretending he is and how willing to take a drink.

[The "Author," presumably, was one Sam Clemens.]

THE OFFENDING BUST stood in a four-man pantheon atop a marble fireplace carved by P. J. Devine, the city's leading marble-cutter, who also had sculpted the small bust of a child ("very meritorious," said the judges) that stands just left of Weller's toga-draped shoulder. Perhaps the sculptor, Pietro Mezzara, California's premiere portraitist of wealthy merchants and partisan politicians, had meant to mitigate Weller's influence by flanking him with two identical plaster casts of the Rev. Mr. Thomas Starr King, the potent abolitionist preacher whose writings and speeches were credited with keeping California on the side of the Union. King had died at thirty-nine, a few months before the exposition, and the memory of his eloquence still stirred the hearts of many San Franciscans, one of whom thought the Mechanics' Fair would be Weller off without Weller.

THE BOTTLE TOWER, a 14-foot octagonal cone of mustard jars, pickle pots, wine bottles, prescription phials, and lamp chimneys, rose in a series of terraces to its crowning bauble, a huge glass carboy filled with acid. This masterpiece of the Pacific Glass Works gave the judges "assurance that the days of dependence on uncertain imported stocks, and the gleanings of the chiffonier, have passed away." [The chiffonier, like imported glass, presumably had originated out-of-state.]

THE GOODIE TABLE, stocked with dozens of samples of chocolate and cocoa cooked up by Domenico Ghirardelli, took top prize in Class XXXVII, "Domestic Preparations." Mark Twain evidenced more interest in a nearby case of pomological, ichthyological and mechanical specimens, including a mean-looking "Catfish Squid" preserved in alcohol, which "when not in liquor and otherwise in good health" could "take a man down and suck him to death."

MARK TWAIN ADVISES
(AND OBSERVES) THE VISITORS
THE 1864 FAIR

September 8, 1864

The ladies should examine some of those rare specimens of embroidery on exhibition at the Mechanics' Fair. Among the finest is a tapestry picture of a royal party in a barge—names "unbeknowns" to us—by W. S. Canan of Healdsburg; a large portrait of G. Washington, by Mrs. Chapman Yates, of San Jose; and a cat and a pile of kittens, by Mrs. Juliana Bayer. We do not like the expression of the old cat's countenance, but the kittens are faultless—especially the blind brown one on the right. So perfectly true to nature are these young cats, that it is easy to see that every school-boy who comes along is seized with an earnest desire to drown them.

September 24, 1864

The children of the Public Schools come in droves and armies to the Fair now, every day, by invitation of the management.... A strong force of Teachers and exhibitors has to be on hand on occasions like these, to keep Young America from being ground up in the machinery.

September 25, 1864

About seventy of the handsomest young ladies in the State marched in double file into the Fair Pavilion yesterday morning.... It was observed that they seemed to take a deeper interest in the pianos and pictures, and especially in the laces and hair-oil and furs, than in the quartz mashers and patent grindstones. It is because their tastes are not fully developed yet, perhaps.

September 30, 1864

It would have worried the good King Herod to see the army of school children that swarmed into the Fair yesterday, if he could have been there to suffer the discomfort of knowing he could not slaughter them under our eccentric system of government without getting himself into trouble.

— Extracts from the *San Francisco Call*

C. E. WATKINS PICTURES THE SCENE

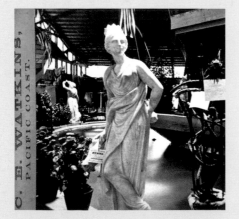

EUROPA, cast in plaster by sculptor Pietro Mezzara, was one of about a dozen life-sized statues around the reflecting pool and fountain at the base of the Floral Tower, wherein reposed the silver brick and the Giant Sanitary Cheese.

THE WINE COUNTER, submitted by R. G. Galien, a dealer in smoking tobacco, chewing tobacco and snuff, displayed boxes of cigars and bottles of California-made claret, all classified in the catalogue as "Food Items."

APPLES, PEARS, GRAPES, figs, plums, pomegranates, quinces, peaches, plums, cherries, blackberries and raspberries spread over half-a-dozen tables in the Horticultural and Botanical Division (XXXIV), Subdivision: Fruit.

THE GOLDEN CITY
IN ITS AGE OF SILVER

1864 The first great boom in Comstock silver stocks collapses as several major mines run into *borrasca* and their inflated value falls by more than 50 percent.

1865 (January 16) Charles and Michael de Young begin free distribution of their impudent handbill, the "Daily Dramatic Chronicle"—later to become the city's longest-lived paper of general circulation, the *San Francisco Chronicle*.

1865 (April 14) President Lincoln is assassinated while attending a theatrical performance in Washington, D.C. The date, by a macabre coincidence, is almost exactly that of the Confederate attack of Fort Sumter four years earlier. In staunchly pro-Union San Francisco, a grieving mob sacks the offices of publications and firms thought to be Southern sympathizers.

1865 With a brass band and fireworks in Union Square, the Mechanics' Institute opens its fifth industrial fair by unveiling a monument to the murdered President. Next morning, the *Alta California* reports: "The statue of Lincoln, larger than life, standing in the centre of the pavilion, under the great dome, elevated almost ten feet above the floor, and placed under a brilliant light, made an imposing appearance. A large chandelier of gas burners, covered by a reflector, illuminated the floor but left the upper part of the dome dark and invisible."

1865 A relatively mild earthquake rattles the city in October. The quake does little damage but inspires a famous cartoon by Edward Jump that makes the whole thing look like great fun.

1866 Consecration of Temple Emanu-El on Sutter Street, now the site of the 450 Sutter medical office building.

1867 Frank Soulé, the polyarticulate co-author of San Francisco's unique historic *Annals*, sometime editor of the leading newspaper (the *Alta California*), one-term State Senator, and dedicatory orator at innumerable holidays, corner-stone-layings and public funerals, reads his rabble-rousing poem "Labor" at the opening of the Mechanics' Fair.

Oh, sons of toil, be proud, look up, arise …
A false society's decrees despise …

THE 1865 EARTHQUAKE was depicted as a merry street party in this cartoon by Edward Jump.

THE NEW HEADQUARTERS were photographed by Eadweard Muybridge, who became famous for his unique, 360-degree panorama of the young city and his kinetographic studies of people and horses in motion. Muybridge was commissioned to make this glass-plate photograph of the new building. The view includes a mound of round cobblestones, awaiting installation in the street, and a gang of curious kids who have gathered to watch the incipient genius at his mysterious work.

1866

MOVING TO POST STREET

Buoyed by a growing membership and the success of its most recent industrial fairs, in 1866 the Mechanics' Institute sold its narrow Italianate street front at 529 California Street, purchased three years earlier for $8500, to the *Alta California* newspaper for almost $80,000. With the proceeds of the sale, the Institute moved boldly southward, out of the heart of the city, to a location on Post Street, between Kearny and Montgomery Streets. The directors hired William Patton, the busiest architect in town, to design the new headquarters—a three-story masonry palace of Venetian and Lombard ancestry. On the street floor were retail shops, lecture halls, "retiring rooms," and a "supper room"; on the second, an open-stack library, men's and women's reading rooms, a chess room and two committee-meeting rooms; on the third, rental space for lodges, scientific organizations or small offices. The Institute remained in its downtown palazzo, despite four decades of almost incessant complaints about its lack of space for books, periodicals, lectures and classes, until April, 1906, when the building and all its contents—including the recently added collections of the Mercantile Library— were destroyed in the firestorm after the great earthquake.

THE WEST END of the main reading room at the new library (1866) offered three tiers of books, upholstered chairs, and potted plants to freshen the air. A narrow stairway (at right) led to the upper gallery.

RACKS OF NEWSPAPERS and periodicals in French, German and English lined the walls of the north reading room, which had Gothic windows and rows of narrow desks for users of reference materials.

THE INSTITUTE AND THE UNIVERSITY: 1868

AN ARRANGED MARRIAGE THAT LASTED A CENTURY

THE CALIFORNIA LEGISLATURE, in granting a charter to the new University of California, made a logical—if unusual—proviso for its governance. It designated the president of the Mechanics' Institute of San Francisco to be a permanent, ex-officio member of the board of regents, thereby sealing a relationship between the Institute and the university that was to endure for 106 years.

In no small measure, this compact between a state university and a membership library recognized and honored one man, Andrew Smith Hallidie, a British-born engineer who ran a thriving business in San Francisco spinning wire rope and building suspension bridges. At that time, Hallidie, who is now remembered primarily as the inventor of the cable car, was an articulate advocate of technical training for young mechanics. He had been a director of the

Mechanics' Institute for several years and had just begun the first of thirteen years as its president.

The charter of the university was written by Hallidie's friend John W. Dwinelle, a San Francisco lawyer, legal scholar and perennial public speaker, who had recently been elected a state assemblyman from Alameda County with the express intent of creating a university and planting it in the East Bay. Dwinelle's bill, adopted by the legislature in 1868, wrapped the College of California, a struggling Congregational school in Oakland, with five students in that year's graduating class, into a broad, non-sectarian institution offering the "arts" of agriculture, mechanics, mining and civil engineering. The governor and the state senate each would appoint eight regents to govern the university. Added to these would be six ex-officio regents: the governor and

ANDREW S. HALLIDIE, 1836–1900, was the most influential leader of the Mechanics' Institute in the nineteenth century. His renown as a public citizen and as inventor of the cable car is recognized in the landmark Hallidie Building at 130 Sutter Street, designed by Willis Polk and built by the University of California in 1918, and Hallidie Plaza, a small park at the foot of Powell Street, where the last cable cars touch Market Street and make their turnaround.

JOHN W. DWINELLE, 1816–1881, historian, lawyer, orator, mayor of Oakland, judge, and regent of the university, specified in the first charter: "… It is expressly provided [that] no sectarian, political or partisan test shall ever be allowed or exercised in the appointment of Regents, or in the election of Professors, teachers, or other officers of the University, or in the admission of students thereto … and persons of every religious denomination, or of no religious denomination, shall be equally eligible to all offices, appointments and scholarships …"

THE INSTITUTE AND THE UNIVERSITY: 1868 *(continued)*

lieutenant governor, the speaker of the assembly and the superintendent of public instruction—plus the head of the California Agricultural Society and the president of the Mechanics' Institute of San Francisco.

Under this charter, Dwinelle became one of the first regents (by appointment), while Hallidie served as a regent during all his many terms as president of the Mechanics' (1868–78 and 1893–95) and also by appointment of various governors from 1876 until his death in 1900.

Hallidie, who had wanted the campus in San Francisco, was displeased with its location in rural Berkeley, but his political success in linking the Mechanics' to the much larger and broader institution not only assured the Institute a voice in the curriculum of the university, but also gave it access to a brilliant new faculty of scientists, historians and literary scholars recruited from around the world. For decades, the Institute's modest building on Post Street served as a San Francisco campus for Berkeley's College of Mechanics. Free lectures by such eminent U.C. professors as Joseph Le Conte, Eugene Hilgard and Ezra Carr usually attracted at least 500 students, the full capacity of the hall, with dozens on a waiting list.

More important to the future of the Institute, in Hallidie's opinion, was his strategy to change its structure from a stockholders' corporation into a nonprofit trust. The stockholders would give up their ownership, the directors would become trustees, and the Institute would become, in effect, a foundation, permitted to seek and accept philanthropic donations. This reform, along with revenue from the industrial fairs (and some timely moves in real estate), saved the Institute from the fate of the Mercantile Library, which eventually starved for lack of community support.

Hallidie never boasted of his role in securing the Mechanics' its position in the governance of the university, but he proudly maintained that the survival of the library was assured on the day in August, 1869, when the stockholders formally accepted his plan, and the Institute "began a new life on a broader and more liberal basis, with increased usefulness to the public and its members."

FAMOUS FACES AND VOICES INAUGURATE THE MECHANICS' TRADITIONAL PUBLIC LECTURES

IT WAS THE first purpose—almost the sacred duty—of mechanics' institutes around the world to offer free or low-priced public lectures on the arts and sciences for the enlightenment of men and women who had had few opportunities for education. When the Mechanics' Institute of San Francisco was less than eight months old, with a small membership and a depleted treasury, the directors enlisted as their first public speaker one the most celebrated orators in America, Edward D. Baker, a former congressman (from Illinois), a future senator (from Oregon), a lawyer for the damned and doomed (in San Francisco) and—at the moment—the most articulate spokesman for the moribund Whig Party and its successor, the infant Republican Party of California.

Baker's speech on the night of November 2, 1855, at the Musical Hall on Bush Street was undoubtedly political and soul-stirring—he could offer nothing else—but it was not among the orations for which he remains famous. Those would include his passionate speeches promoting the nascent Republican Party in its stand against the spread of slavery; his eulogy over the coffin of Senator David C. Broderick, whose death in a duel Baker blamed on Broderick's anti-slavery position; and his dramatic appearance in full army uniform, with sword in hand, in the United States Senate in 1861, just after the Union defeat at the first Battle of Bull Run, to denounce a fellow-senator who had urged abandoning the war. Baker, a colonel in the Union Army as well as a senator, died in action less than three months later in the Battle of Ball's Bluff.

Lack of money and membership, as well as the distraction of war, silenced the Institute's public lectures for several years. But with the infusion of Comstock money into San Francisco and the backing of a

EDWARD D. BAKER
Famed as a politician, he died as a soldier.

JOSIAH DWIGHT WHITNEY
He surveyed California's peaks and hollows.

WILLIAM H. BREWER
He wrote the book on the great geo survey.

THOMAS STARR KING
He made the moral case for abolition.

WILLIAM C. RALSTON
He was the venture capitalist of the infant city.

wealthy patron, the banker William Ralston, the Institute again offered a series of lectures in October, 1863. These presented to the republic of workmen three of the most articulate and influential men of their time: the Rev. Mr. Thomas Starr King, the founder of the First Unitarian Church of San Francisco and one of the nation's most passionate abolitionist orators; the State Geologist Josiah Whitney, a distinguished geological and mineral scientist, who was then in the midst of his scrupulous, eight-year-long survey of California geography and geology; and Professor William H. Brewer, one of the first graduates of Yale University's renowned Sheffield Scientific School, who was serving as Whitney's chief assistant—and whose informal journal is a classic publication in California history and geography.

In the 1870s, prospering from membership dues and the revenues of its annual industrial fairs, the Institute began offering courses in such subjects as "Drawing and Linear Perspective" and individual lectures, usually by university professors, in such subjects as "The Air We Breathe," "Pioneers of American Civilization," "The Mathematics of Mining," "Explosives," and the economic and political issue that haunted California for almost a century: "The Chinese Question." The lecture series brought to San Francisco many of the most popular teachers from the University of California's Berkeley campus, which had become a source of academic supply for the Mechanics' Institute. Professor Joseph Le Conte of U.C., the Harvard-trained geologist whose passion for fieldwork made him one of the most intense students of the mountain West—especially of Yosemite National Park—gave several series of lectures, as did Ezra S. Carr, the first professor of agriculture at Berkeley. Dr. Carr, an advocate of practical, hands-on experience for future farmers, and reigning scholar of the "Patrons of Agriculture" (the Grange movement), returned to the Mechanics' year after year, as did his successor as head of agricultural studies at U.C., Dr. Eugene W. Hilgard.

A PAIR OF TOWERS *(no dome)* ON UNION SQUARE

THE MECHANICS' fourth exhibit hall—the largest, most conspicuous, most heavily used to date—rose in a few breathless weeks of July on the southeast corner of Union Square. The neighborhood was becoming the city's most fashionable place to pray. Three major congregations, each founded during the gold rush, had moved or were moving to new edifices on or near the Square: Calvary Presbyterian Church, on the Powell Street side (where the St. Francis Hotel stands today); Trinity Episcopal Church on the northwest corner (later the site of the Fitzhugh Building and, more recently, of Saks Fifth Avenue); and, up on the hill at what is now 450 Sutter Street, the twin-towered synagogue of Congregation Emanu-El.

By no accident, the façade of the new Mechanics' Pavilion looked like a small, mirror-image of Temple Emanu-El. Both buildings were the work of the same architect, William Patton, a roving Englishman who had tossed aside his career as an architect to pan for gold in California in 1849. After a decade of mining, peddling, painting and occasional contracting, Patton had come back to San Francisco and almost immediately became a leading architect. (The Mechanics' Library, built in 1866 at 31 Post Street, was among his many commissions.)

Patton, a non-Jew, may have been inspired by pictures or reports of the 3000-seat, twin-towered synagogue that another non-Jewish architect, Otto Wagner, of Vienna, had

designed nine years earlier, in 1859, for the Dohnayi Street congregation of Budapest, one of the largest and wealthiest congregations in Europe. In any case, Patton's scheme for Temple Emanu-El echoed the basilical structure and cathedral-like towers of Wagner's masterpiece—and the Mechanics' new pavilion on Union Square, built for a little less than $45,000, was a beneficiary of this inspiration.

Opened in mid-August, the Sixth Industrial Fair ran for five weeks (Admission, 50 cents; Season ticket for a Gentleman and Lady, $5; Season Ticket for a Single, $3). On display, along with the usual water pumps, steam engines and horse blankets, was the first railroad sleeping car to be shipped out west in anticipation of the opening next year of the great transcontinental line.

A few days after the Fair closed, the Pavilion was open again for a Carnival Costume Ball, the grandest social event of the fall season. The water in the central fountain was spiked with perfume. The ceiling was hung with garlands of greenery, bunches of flowers, and fully inhabited canary cages and goldfish bowls.

"The night was clear and the great Square flooded with moonlight, as carriage after carriage rolled up to the entrance and discharged its precious freight of 'fair women and brave men,'" the weekly *Golden City* reported. A man dressed as a "Wild Irishman" won top prize for costume. It was reported that he played his role "to the life."

THE FOURTH PAVILION echoes Temple Emanu-El, seen in the background at right.

THE UNION DEMOCRAT

| VOLUME XV | SONORA, TUOLUMNE COUNTY, AUGUST 22, 1868 | NUMBER 11 |

An exclusive letter to the Gold Country's leading daily from reporter J. N. Stone at the Fair in San Francisco

AUGUST 11, 1868

EDITOR DEMOCRAT:—The Sixth Industrial Fair of the Mechanics' Institute opened about mid-day of Saturday last. In the evening there was a great display of rockets at the front on Stockton street, and a great tooting of horns....

The Pavilion—if such an immense structure can be properly so called—is lighted by about 1400 gas burners. The *"Mechanics' Fair Daily Press,"* of which I send you the latest copy, calls it 1200, but they make a number of errors to my certain knowledge. On Monday, (yesterday), the steam Engines were put in motion. There was one little Engine, the entire cylinder of which is in length not more than six, and the stroke of its piston about four inches, that worked with such quickness that the eye could scarcely catch its motion.... This little steam engine was built by a youth named Robert Blair in the first year of his apprenticeship [*at the Vulcan Foundry of Daniel Van Pelt, one of the first directors of the Mechanics' Institute*]. The engines are all placed inside the main building; but the furnaces and steam boilers are in a separate adjoining building.

Sewing machines, and the fabrics they are used upon, are largely represented. Cutlery, mechanics' tools, saws of every description and brass foundry work, all manufactured in our State, make considerable display, but what attracted my attention most were the beautiful woolen fabrics, which gave promise that the Pacific world was destined to rival all the world in the manufacture of wool. There is great variety of these including the finest and heaviest blankets and flannels I ever saw. I noticed also some heavy cloths, similar to the English and French Beaver, which for softness of material, evenness and beauty of finish, ought to satisfy a fastidious taste, if made into gentlemen's apparel. Also for ladies' wear, a very large assortment of heavy figured woolen stuffs, generally with light ground and small spotted figure, such as are worn in sacks or jackets, were quite noticeable as exhibiting the skill and progress in wool manufactures in this new world.... When one sees so many evidences of Art and fine mechanism in one grand collection—all produced in our midst—one can scarcely believe that California has risen up so gracefully and symmetrically from its barbarous cradle of twenty years ago.

It is a very pleasant sight to ascend to the gallery, and, standing at the eastern end, to gaze down upon the scene when lighted by gas-light. The countless jets of light, stretching along in rows on either side and enclosing a vista of nearly 300 feet in length, is a sight both novel and pleasing. In the very midst the fountain is seen with three principal jets of clear sparkling water; the center jet throwing its perpendicular column from 20 to 25 feet and descending in a glittering spray into the basin below. Near by a Gordon power press, carried by belting from the main shaft, is operating in the printing of the last remaining page of the *"Mechanics' Fair Daily Press"* (it being the first page) and as fast as it is printed it is distributed among the curious waiting crowd.

Then, in congregated array, we behold the gorgeous display of many fineries; the view embracing the whole vast collection, enriched to the sight by its endless variety. And there, through the meandering passageways, moves the crowd. There are men, there are boys and girls; there are even some old ladies; but there are likewise some fair, beautiful women in just the beautiful time of life, who, whilst gliding through that brilliant place seem, no doubt, to the young bloods like houris of a fairyland, or like the nymphs of paradise.

In addition to what is contained in the large room of the Pavilion a great variety of pianos, melodeons, etc., occupy the north-east room at the front, its dimensions being 35 by 60 feet; while the south-east room of the same size contains the well supplied Fair Restaurant; and visitors from the country, if they choose, need have no occasion to quit the pavilion grounds, except to seek their lodgings or make their toilet.

At the west end is the ... Picture Gallery. The room is 205 feet long and 30 feet wide. The principal Photographists [*sic*] of the city here make their display of pictures including sun pearls and stereoscopic views. Portraits and landscape painters are quite extensively represented.... All the painting, I thought, looked very well by gas light and at a certain distance. In fact, with some of them, "distance lends enchantment to the view." ...

At night, the entire Pavilion is so well lighted by gas, that one can read the finest print; and by day, the sunlight (sometimes—when it ain't foggy) streams through nearly 800 sashes or about 5000 glass panes.

1868

THE SIXTH
INDUSTRIAL FAIR

THE GREAT WALL OF WATKINS, in the picture gallery of the Mechanics' Fair in 1868, displayed many of Carleton E. Watkins's already-famous glass-plate views of Yosemite Valley, the Sierra and the Willamette Valley. Watkins' mastery of the still-experimental medium gained him a bronze medal at the international exposition in Paris that year and a gold medal at the Mechanics' Industrial Fair. Prints, books and stereographs of Watkins's landscapes, sold from his studio on Montgomery Street, became fixtures in countless homes, offices and hotel lobbies. By publicizing the beauties of the West, Watkins created public interest that led to the establishment of California's first state park, incorporated into Yosemite National Park in 1905.

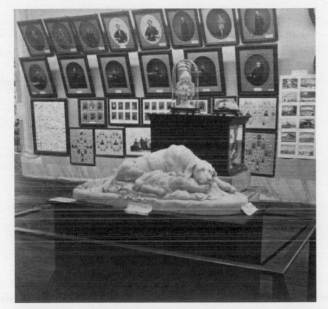

A GRIEVING PARENT'S MONUMENT to a dead child, guarded by a mournful spaniel, moved some visitors to tears. The usually acerbic reviewer for the *San Francisco News-Letter* called the marble statue by Pietro Mezzara (commissioned by the child's father, Edwin Davis) "a beautiful and touching thing," a gem in Mezzara's "truly excellent collection." As for the rest of the exhibit, the critic (could it have been the *News-Letter*'s new editor, Ambrose Bierce?) rated the paintings "not creditable" and the photography trite: "Watkins and others of the scenery men have the customary exhibition of Yosemite and Columbia River."

MEDALLIONS FORE AND AFT decorated the back of Carleton E. Watkins's stereopticon views of Western landscapes, city scenes and Mechanics' industrial fairs published after 1868. Watkins's good friend William Keith, who was later to become the most prestigious and wealthy painter of panoramic landscapes on the West Coast, contrived the design with snaky lines, a lavish sampling of typefaces and a neo-Roman profile of France's late-blooming imperialist Louis-Napoléon Bonaparte, goateed, laurel-crowned and fated to be deposed in a couple of years.

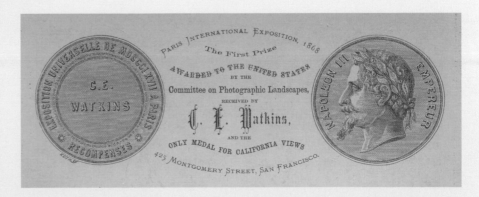

MARK TWAIN SHOWS THE MERCANTILE LIBRARY HOW TO PACK A HALL

BACK IN SAN FRANCISCO after a year and a half of lecturing in the East, and sending articles about his travels in Europe to the *Alta California*, the leading newspaper of the Far West, Mark Twain was raring for a new audience in his old stamping grounds. The Mercantile Association, which had just moved into a stylish, costly, mortgage-haunted new headquarters on Bush Street, hired him to speak on any of the myriad subjects that now intrigued him. Twain chose "Venice: Past and Present," which he had visited a few months before and was to describe in his forthcoming book *The Innocents Abroad* as "forlorn and beggared, forgotten of the world."

In the book, his first best-seller, Twain devoted three chapters to Venice. He found much to admire in its art and architecture and little to praise in its current state. Presumably this material, spiced with his measured wit and cornpone delivery, made up most of his speech at the Mercantile on July 2, 1868. A reporter for the *Alta*, who covered the event in detail, noted that the talk had lasted an hour and fifty minutes ("though it was not a minute too long"), and that Twain had compared Venice in the unkind light of day to "Sacramento when overflowed." (Sacramento's notorious propensity to flood was well known in those days to all Californians, and was a standard base for regional jokes.) The *Alta*'s competitor, the *Daily Examiner*, called the speech "a perfect success both in a literary and financial point," which is precisely what the speaker and the Mercantile were praying for.

Twain, who had no peer save P. T. Barnum in chumming fish to his net, had written and caused to be published an "open letter" to himself, pleading with him to abandon his plan to read a chapter or two of his book in public.

"There is a limit to human endurance," wrote the alleged signers of the letter, including Twain's good friend Bret Harte, Major-General E.O.C. Ord, Citizens on Foot and Horseback, and 1500 in the Steerage. "We urge you to desist from this new atrocity you contemplate."

Twain followed this with warnings from the "Pacific Board of Brokers [and other financial and social institutions], the Proprietors of the *Alta*, *Bulletin*, *Times*, *Call*, *Examiner* [and other San Francisco publications], THE CLERGY, and THE CHIEF OF POLICE" and wound up with a defiant ad:

ADMISSION—ONE DOLLAR. Doors open at 7. Orgies to commence at 8 P.M. The public displays and ceremonies projected to give fitting éclat to this occasion have been unavoidably delayed until the 4th. The lecture will be delivered certainly on the 2nd, and the event will be celebrated two days afterward by a discharge of artillery on the 4th, a procession of citizens, the reading of the Declaration of Independence, and by a glorious display of fireworks from Russian Hill in the evening, which I have ordered at my sole expense, the cost amounting to eighty thousand dollars.

Twain gently teased his audience by thanking them for attending in defiance of "such a widespread, such a furious, such a determined opposition to my lecturing upon this occasion," and he apologized for making the lecture "somewhat didactic."

"I don't know what didactic means," he said, "but it is a good, high-sounding word, and I wish to use it, meaning no harm whatever."

The harmless, somewhat didactic lecture added a notch to Twain's growing fame and brought some desperately needed cash to the Mercantile Association. It would be a long time before another rescuer such as Twain came to their debt-encumbered platform.

THE FAULT RUMBLES
AND LITERARY LIONS ROAR

1868 A severe earthquake jolts the Bay Area, "the most severe felt here since the foundation of the Mission ninety-two years ago," the daily *Alta California* reports on October 21. "The main facts of the earthquake as felt in this city, are that four persons were killed by the falling of cornices and chimneys, that a dozen brick buildings on made ground are shattered so that they are untenantable; that the cornices of two buildings have been thrown down, and many walls cracked, much plastering loosened and many window panes broken."

1869 The joining of the tracks of the Central Pacific and Union Pacific Railroads in Utah completes the long-awaited railroad link between the West and East Coasts, but the expected boon to California's unbalanced, infant economy turns into a drain as lower-priced manufactures from the East invade the Western markets.

1870 San Francisco designates its first great public open space, hires William Hammond Hall to survey more than 1000 acres of sand dunes, scrub brush and squatters' cottages and plan a garden for this dismal beach land, now called "Golden Gate Park."

1871 News of the outbreak of war between France and Prussia (April) excites the anxieties of San Francisco's large French and German communities. In the huge Mechanics' Pavilion on Union Square, a French "Sanitary Fair" to raise money for medical relief in Europe is followed a week or two later by a German "Sanitary Fair" for the same purpose.

AMBROSE BIERCE

BIERCE AND HARTE

San Francisco's literary "golden era"— a brief period of local creativity and cultural independence between the Civil War and the completion of the railroad link to the Atlantic Coast, came to full boil in 1868 with the appointment of Ambrose Bierce, twenty-six, as editor and columnist for Frederick Marriott's weekly *San Francisco News-Letter* and Bret Harte, thirty-six, as editor of Anton Roman's new *Overland Monthly*. Bierce immediately began scolding and vilifying his enemies in his "Town Crier" column, a self-imposed task he con-

BRET HARTE

tinued for more than forty years on various publications. Harte, along with publishing Mark Twain and other of his literary buddies, saw into print his classic tales of gold rush California: "The Luck of Roaring Camp" and "The Outcasts of Poker Flat"—and, two years later, his widely quoted and unfortunately widely misunderstood satire "Plain Language from Truthful James" (also called "The Heathen Chinee"), in which two unscrupulous gamblers complain of being outwitted by another card-sharp who happens to be Chinese.

AN AIRSHIP FLIES AT MECHANICS' HALL

A few weeks before the scheduled opening of the Mechanics' Seventh Industrial Fair in mid-August, 1869, Frederick Marriott—editor, publisher, entrepreneur, town scold and would-be aviator—brought the most peculiar, fanciful and exciting contrivance ever seen in San Francisco—maybe *anywhere*—into the twin-towered pavilion on Union Square. It was a self-propelled, steam-powered, navigable flying machine—or, rather, a scaled-down, test model of such a machine—and it actually flew. Marriott had built it with thousands of hours of his own time and thousands of his own dollars and had dubbed it, for want of a name for its species, the *Avitor Hermes Jr.*

The Avitor, which has been variously described as 27, 28 or 37 feet long, was essentially a gas bag, shaped like a huge sweet potato, with a couple of rudimentary wings, an adjustable rudder and a small, alcohol-burning steam engine that drove two propellers. Marriott had flown it like a giant, motor-driven kite at a race course in San Mateo County in July, shortly before he brought it to the Mechanics' Pavilion to show it to the doubters as well as the potential backers of his visionary airline, the Aerial Steam Navigation Company. Marriott's company, incorporated three years earlier with an infusion of cash from the risk-friendly banker Billy Ralston, proposed to launch a fleet of full-scale, passenger-carrying dirigibles, San Francisco to New York, to compete with the just-completed transcontinental railroad.

"The morning was beautiful and still—scarcely a breath of air stirring," wrote a reporter from the *San Francisco Times* who witnessed the first flight at Shell Mound Track, on the flats beside the bay. "In six minutes steam was got up—the rudder set to give a slight curve to the course of the vessel—and the valves opened. With the first turn of the propellers she rose until the rate of five miles an hour was attained. The position of the rudder caused her to describe a great circle, around which she passed twice, occupying about five minutes each time. Lines had been fastened to both bow and stern, which were held by two men who followed her track and had sufficient ado to keep up with her at a 'dog trot.'"

The *Scientific American* reprinted this report, but observed that no engine existed that would be light enough and strong enough to propel a massive sausage, filled with hydrogen and weighted with passengers, from coast to coast. Marriott shrugged off this skepticism, launched his model Avitor twice a day inside the Mechanics' Pavilion (much the biggest indoor space in San Francisco) and sold an unrecorded number of adult admissions at 50 cents and kids at 25.

In the hard times of the 1870s, Marriott's aerial navigation company deflated after the demo period, but the inventor never lost his vigor for his cause. English-born, Marriott had apprenticed in London's sarcastic school of newspaper writing, and he made profitable use of his penmanship in San Francisco in what he called "rattlesnake journalism." While mocking his rivals in his weekly *News-Letter and Commercial Advertiser,* he relentlessly publicized his aviation project. He hustled innumerable friends, including Mark Twain, down to the basement of the Montgomery Block to see the Avitor in construction; persuaded Bret Harte to write a poem about the aircraft; and petitioned the Board of Supervisors for $19,000 in damages for letting a mob, grieving for Abraham Lincoln, trash

the *News-Letter* office in revenge for Marriott's Confederate sympathies. Marriott pledged to spend the money building a full-sized Avitor.

The *Hermes Jr.* exploded and burned soon after its debut, leaving only a few pictures and designs. Marriott is remembered, if at all, not as the man who created America's first dirigible but as the publisher who hired Ambrose Bierce as editor in 1868 and unleashed his blistering column "The Town Crier" on the startled city.

THE AVITOR HERMES JR., floating shoulder-high at Shell Mound Track in July, 1869, flew later at the Mechanics' Fair but did not compete for a medal. There was no category for flying machines.

THE DEBT-RIDDEN MERCANTILE PLANS A CLASSY FUNDRAISER

For several years, the Mercantile Association, the upscale rival of the Mechanics' Institute, had been struggling to pay for its handsome new building in the heart of the downtown business district. The trustees had spent $50,000 for the site—an abandoned cemetery, right next door to the Calvary Presbyterian Church on the north side of Bush Street between Montgomery and Sansome Streets—and they had hired the most successful architect in town, David Farquharson, to design a four-story office block with mansard roof, arched windows, sculptured columns, and a crown of wrought-iron frets. The contractors worked in fits and starts while the debt on the project swelled to $236,000, a staggering burden on an organization with annual revenues of less than $18,000. Bravely, the trustees staged an official opening and booked public lectures by such popular figures as Mark Twain, but the Association was nearly bankrupt. First, they tried to issue $100,000 in bonds, but they could not find a buyer, even at 9 percent interest. A subscription drive produced no subscriptions, and a membership drive produced few members. A course of lectures by "Eastern orators of distinguished reputation" failed to attract an audience (Twain's talk excepted) and the fees paid to the distinguished Eastern orators further depleted the shrinking treasury.

In his annual report for 1867, the president, William H. L. Barnes, a conspicuous public figure, lawyer and military leader, complained: "We expected criticism of the location selected, of the plan adopted, of the building erected, and of the temerity which would incur so large a liability upon apparently slender resources; and I feel bound to say, that in this respect at least, our expectations have not been disappointed."

The project was kept alive for a couple of years by a substantial loan from the French Savings and Loan Society and an even larger advance from the Bank of California, under the venturesome leadership of William Ralston, who happened to be a trustee of the Association as well as president of the bank. But, as the new building neared completion, the French Savings and Loan, having collected no interest, lost patience and foreclosed its $95,000 loan. The sheriff stood by to auction off the property at a public sale.

"Just as the hearts of the Trustees were most faint and weary, temporary relief came from an unexpected quarter," wrote Robert B. Swain, the upright citizen who had succeeded Col. Barnes in the unhappy job of president. The "temporary relief" was not unlike that brought to the failing Mechanics' Institute fourteen years earlier by the actress Julia Dean Hayne. In this case, the heroine was a brilliant young violinist, Camilla Urso, who happened to be looking for a sponsor and a venue for an appearance in San Francisco. The arrangements fell together before the sheriff could drop his gavel. Billy Ralston agreed to pay off the French S&L and extend his own loans to keep the Association afloat until Mlle Urso could bring her show to town. As for an appropriate location for a huge, fund-raising event, what could be more convenient, more expandable, more available than the vast Mechanics' Pavilion on Union Square?

THE ROMAN-TEMPLE FAÇADE of Calvary Presbyterian Church was dwarfed by the four-story Mercantile Library designed by David Farquharson and his partner, Henry Kenitzer. The church moved uptown to Union Square a year later, and its old space was filled by a new building that, in turn, dwarfed the Mercantile Library.

A "DEMORALIZING" GIFT CONCERT TOPS CAMILLA'S MODEST YIELD

TEN THOUSAND music lovers, seated or standing, attended the first concert of the "Great Music Festival" at the Mechanics' Pavilion on an evening late in February, 1870. Mayor Thomas H. Selby bought the Grand Box for $3200. (Selby, the owner of the major smelter for the mines of the Comstock Lode, was a patron and sometime trustee of the Mechanics' Library as well as a life-member of the Mercantile.) At the second, reduced-price concert, fifteen thousand crowded in, and thousands more attended on the third and fourth days.

At each performance they heard some of the most popular ceiling-busters of that era: the Hallelujah Chorus of Handel's *Messiah*, sung by a choir of 1500 adults and 3000 children; Carl Maria von Weber's *Jubilee Overture* (1818); and the "Anvil Chorus" from Verdi's *Il Trovatore*, performed by an orchestra of 300 instruments. At last came the chef d'oeuvre, Mlle Urso, herself, playing Beethoven's *Violin Concerto in D Major* and, as an encore, *The Last Rose of Summer*.

On the fifth day, the Mercantile Library put on a Grand Ball, a benefit for Mlle Urso. The cavernous main hall was lighted by 1200 gas jets (or maybe 1500—there never was agreement as to the number of gas jets at the Mechanics' Pavilion) and decorated with the now-familiar garlands of flowers and cages of canaries dangling from the ceiling (about all you could afford to do in a space like that).

The Urso concerts netted $12,250, enough to assure the Mercantile another year of life, but scarcely a nip in its massive debt. The only hope of saving the Mercantile from losing everything—its books, its building and its position as the leading library of the West—lay in a series of three "Gift Concerts" specially authorized by the state legislature as a permissible breach of California's strict ban on gambling games.

The "gift concerts" were, of course, lotteries. Every admission ticket to the first and richest "concert" carried a number to be entered in a series of drawings for $500,000 in cash prizes, from $100 (there would be 425 of those) up to $100,000 (just one). People all over the United States bought tickets, and on the day of the first "concert," about fifteen thousand expectant winners crowded into the Pavilion.

By year's end, the three Gift Concerts had returned a profit of $333,290. The Mechanics' Institute collected $155,000 for canceling its autumn fair and lending its Pavilion to the cause. The Mercantile paid off its debts and settled into its new headquarters with sighs of relief accompanied by pangs of guilt for pandering to San Francisco's most notorious weakness—the greed for easy money, the rage for instant gain.

The Mercantile's President Swain, a prominent churchman, philanthropist (and sometime director of the U.S. Mint), confessed in his annual report: "Thus was the Institution, by a process at once corrupting and demoralizing—a process which it may be hoped for the honor of the people will not be repeated in the State—saved from the jaws of death."

BORN IN FRANCE, the prodigy Camilla Urso had been brought to the United States at age ten by her Italian father (a flutist) and her Portuguese mother (a singer) to make her first concert tour in 1852. The family later settled in Nashville, Tennessee, where Camilla continued her musical training. By the time of her concert series at the Mechanics' Pavilion she had reached the ripe age of twenty-eight, had formed her own concert company, and had become a master of the violin, an instrument that long was considered an unassailably masculine property.

A DAY OF SUDDEN RICHES

(for a few)

*For months our citizens have been in an unnatural state of excitement over the grand
scheme projected by the Mercantile Library to extricate their property from debt.
It was a Gift Concert, vulgarly called lottery, of the most gigantic proportions.*
—*Alta California*, Nov. 1, 1870

The grand scheme was simple. The Mercantile would sell 200,000 tickets, priced at $5 in gold coin, and would give back $500,000 in prizes. After expenses, the net should pay all debts and leave a few dollars to spend on books. Daily newspaper ads reminded the public that the "Grand Gift Concert" was permitted only by a *Special Act of the Legislature*. Such a chance to get rich in a day would never, ever occur again in the law-abiding State of California.

An hour before the doors of the Mechanics' Pavilion opened at 8 A.M. the streets were thronged with anxious-looking men and women. It was a Monday, but nobody wanted to go to work. Up on stage in the main hall were the city's most conspicuous wielders of wealth and power, standing guard over several large, sealed boxes holding 200,000 numbered leather tags and 628 small, gilded boxes. Each little box contained a roll of paper printed with a sum from $100 to $100,000. The presidents of all the leading banks (the Wells Fargo, the London & San Francisco, the Hibernia, the Bank of California), the mayor, the supervisors, the leaders of bench and bar, were there to certify the integrity of the proceedings. At either side of the stage stood a large tumbler wheel, one for the numbers, one for the boxes. To guarantee a fair draw, the management had recruited six boys and six girls, certified to be totally blind, from the Asylum for the Deaf, Dumb and Blind to draw the boxes and the tickets. Stage left, a child would draw a number and hand it to a caller. Stage right, another child would draw a gilded box. A caller would cut open the box, hand the roll of paper to the child, who would unfold it and pass it to another caller to be read. Every half hour or so, they would give the blind children a break and rotate the callers.

The first draw, at ten o'clock, brought a prize of $19,000. The crowd screamed with excitement. The second number won $1,000. More cheers. The third drew $100 and a burst of laughter.

All morning the wheels turned, disposing of fifty to sixty prizes an hour. Two orchestras alternated playing in the Art Gallery, and the sightless boys and girls dipped their bare hands into the tumblers again and again. On the one-hundred-and-ninety-first draw, Number 154,077 came up. The corresponding gift box was worth $100,000.

"The crowd sprang to their feet, whooping and halloing," the *Alta* reported. An elderly Irish woman was dragged to the stage, where she pleaded "not guilty" of owning the prize. Then rumors fixed upon a storekeeper named S. W. Lederer, but he, too, was not guilty. Finally, the winning number was traced to an agent named Jacob Levy who had sold a batch of 105 tickets for $500 to Isidor Wormser, a broker with William Meyer & Co. Wormser happened to be among the fifty or so leading citizens up on the platform to certify the integrity of the proceedings, but he did not jump with joy. It turned out he had re-sold his tickets to a four-man gambling syndicate assembled by a brother in New York.

The drawings continued, hour after hour, until nearly midnight. Western Union incessantly telegraphed the winning numbers to Chicago and New York and to newspapers in many states. The *Alta* put out an extra edition every twenty minutes. Around the bulletin board outside Western Union, several citizens had their pockets picked.

When the last gilded box had been drawn and cut open, and the last number (a $500 winner) had been read aloud and posted by the callers, Robert Swain, the president of the Association, came onstage and apologized for the "peculiar process of this undertaking ... the best and the only salvation for the Mercantile Library."

The salvation did not endure. Two more Gift Concerts, paltry little dollar-a-ticket affairs, with grand pianos as the top prizes, followed. Like Camilla's violin, they did not bring in much money. Two years later, the Mercantile Association had less than $20,000 in its treasury. Members were already complaining about the location, the lighting, the book shelves, and the cost of the beautiful new library, so dearly bought. Looking back, one can see that the Grand Gift Concert was perhaps the greatest moment of the Mercantile Library, but also the beginning of its end.

THE WEALTH AND RANCOR OF THE "TERRIBLE SEVENTIES"

B y a cruel paradox, the completion of the first transcontinental railroad not only failed to bring California the expected surge of prosperity, but marked instead the beginning of a deep and general depression that continued through the whole of the next decade. A frustrated and embittered populace blamed its disappointment and sufferings on the railroad and on the Chinese. Thus the difficulties of a long period of economic distress were aggravated by racial antagonism and political upheaval.

—Walton Bean in *California: An Interpretive History*

1870 San Francisco's city government launches a systematic persecution of Chinese residents with ordinances forbidding the carrying of buckets attached to poles laid across the shoulders and outlawing the rental of sleeping rooms with less than 500 cubic feet of air space per occupant.

1871 San Francisco newspaper editor Henry George begins publishing editorials and pamphlets developing the economic theories incorporated later in his international best-seller *Progress and Poverty*, advocating an end to speculation in land by imposing a single tax of 100 percent on the "unearned increment" in the sale price.

1871 Artists, writers and students meet at the Mechanics' Institute to found an association that ultimately becomes the San Francisco Art Institute.

1872 (June 18) A Woman's Suffrage Convention, one of the first in the nation—and certainly the first in California—meets at the Mercantile Library.

1873 The Modoc War, a bloody, treacherous and ultimately tragic encounter between the United States Army and the tribal peoples of California, ends with the rebels' surrender after a prolonged resistance to the forced movement of Klamath and Modoc tribes near the Oregon-California border.

1873 In the midst of national depression, the bonanza silver mines of the Comstock Lode around Virginia City, Nevada, set off a new round of wild stock speculation in San Francisco.

1873 Levi Strauss, an immigrant from Bavaria who had established a business in San Francisco manufacturing and selling men's work clothes in 1850, takes out a patent with his business associate Jacob W. Davis on a style of men's denim jeans fastened at the strain points with copper rivets.

1873 American stock markets suddenly lose more than $200 million in panic selling. Thousands are out of work. The crisis tests the administration of Ulysses S. Grant with bankruptcies, scandals and grievous poverty in cities throughout America.

A NEW UNITED STATES MINT (later to become the "Old" Mint) was under construction at Fifth and Mission Streets from 1870 to 1874, when the government took official possession. Construction had reached the first level of granite blocks when the ubiquitous photographer Eadweard Muybridge recorded the work-in-progress.

MR. HALLIDIE UNVEILS THE TRANSIT OF THE FUTURE

ANDREW S. HALLIDIE WAS one of the rare San Franciscans who had actually made his start as a miner in the gold rush. Up in Calaveras County, he recalled, he had earned "three or four dollars a week—just enough to starve on, with beans, pork, and coffee, and pork, coffee, and beans for a change." For several years he had drifted from one mining camp to another, applying his muscles to digging and sluicing gravel, without seeing much gold. Eventually, his skill as a mechanic—and his boyhood training as the son of a Scottish engineer with patents on the spinning of virtually indestructible, multistrand wire cables—found application in a wire suspension bridge that he designed and built on the American River, and in a wire rope system he devised to raise and lower ore carts at a quartz mine on a steep slope above the stream.

With his handmade machinery and his experience in the gold country, Hallidie came down to San Francisco in 1857 and opened a small factory below Telegraph Hill to manufacture wire rope. In the next ten years, he made a modest living and an international reputation designing, manufacturing and erecting wire suspension bridges, meanwhile taking out many patents for ropeway or tramway systems to transport ore and other heavy materials in the mountainous West.

Hallidie's enthusiasm for the practical use of technical education made him one of the most successful advocates of the Mechanics' Institute in the nineteenth century—and one of the most prominent exhibitors at many Mechanics' Fairs. A correspondent for *Scientific American* reported on his 1869 display: "A suspension bridge connects the galleries near the fountain, and enlightens the otherwise ignorant as to the modes of making and using wire cables.... The bridge is the joy of all juvenile and many senile visitors."

The hills of San Francisco challenged him. In a lecture at the Mechanics' Institute, Hallidie described his obsession with creating a system of underground cables to move streetcars:

> *I was largely induced to think over the matter from seeing the difficulty and pain the horses experience in hauling the cars up Jackson Street, from Kearny to Stockton Street, on which street four or five horses were needed for the purpose—the driving being accompanied by the free use of the whip and voice, and occasionally by the horses falling and being dragged down the hill on their sides, by the car loaded with passengers sliding on its track.*

As his plans matured, Hallidie enlisted three friends—fellow trustees of the Mechanics' Institute—to help raise money for a trial line. His backers were Joseph Britton, of the lithographers Britton & Rey; James Moffitt, of the paper wholesalers Blake, Moffitt & Towne; and a former sheriff, Henry L. Davis, who later served as treasurer of the Institute.

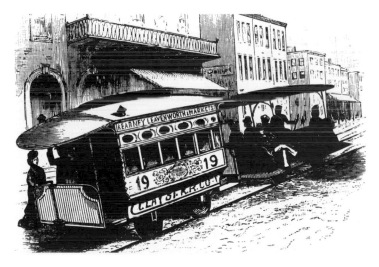

SOON AFTER THE TRIAL RUN (August 2, 1873) of Hallidie's "wire rope street railway" on the slippery slope of Clay Street from Kearny to Jones, the invention began to be admired—and imitated—around the world, sometimes with a grip system that infringed on Hallidie's hard-bought patents. This drawing, based on a photograph, gave the readers of *Harper's Weekly* their first view of the Clay Street car-and-dummy, with passengers inside and out.

The company obtained a franchise from the city, but the local newspapers and other purveyors of doubt were skeptical. Disappointed by a paltry sale of stock and a feeble show of pledges from would-be capitalists, Hallidie came up with $20,000 of his limited money; persuaded his three associates from the Mechanics' Institute to invest about $40,000; and found a banker (former mayor Ephraim W. Burr) who would lend $30,000 for ten years at 10 percent interest, with a mortgage on the unbuilt railroad as security.

THE GEARY STREET CABLE carried a heavy load of passengers from downtown to the Western Addition, the fashionable residential district west of Van Ness Avenue.

To the riders who ventured, first timidly, then boldly, to ride Mr. Hallidie's "wire rope street railway" up and down the Clay Street hill, the breezy little passenger cars were scary, fun, mysterious and almost miraculous.

The *Mining & Scientific Press, Harper's Weekly* and *Leslie's Illustrated Weekly* printed diagrams, cross-section drawings and steel engravings of San Francisco's strange new horseless trolleys and of the patented grip that allowed the operator to attach and detach the car from a moving cable without slipping downhill. In truth, the grip was only a novel application of a device Hallidie and others had used in hauling ore carts and other heavy loads with wire cables. It was the slot in the street, enclosing the cable and preventing its interfering with other traffic, that was key to the system—the one part that Hallidie did not patent.

Hallidie dwelt on the importance of the narrow slot in a description of the system written for *Scientific American* (1881):

The system consists of an endless wire rope [not really endless *but looped] placed in a tube below the surface of the ground, between the tracks of a railroad, and kept in position by means of sheaves, upon and beneath which the rope is kept in motion by a stationary engine, the power being transmitted from the motor to the rope by means of a grip or other suitable pulleys, and from the rope to the cars*

on the street by means of a gripping bar … which passes through a narrow slot in the upper side of the tube.

Hallidie, always eager to sell wire rope, pointed out that cable cars worked on level lines as well as hills and could push their own snow plows in wintry climates. In San Francisco, his Clay Street line had been only the beginning. Within a few years, the Sutter Street Railroad Company, "whose lines had for many years been unprofitably worked by horses," had put in three miles of cable tracks. The California Street Railroad built a line that crested two major hills, and the Geary Street Railroad ran a relatively level line through the most populous area of the city.

"The wear and tear on the streets, as well as the accumulation of filth due to horses, is entirely avoided," Hallidie observed.

By the early 1890s, there were 25 miles of track in San Francisco, eight cable car companies and 208 cars. Passengers made more than two thousand round trips daily. Cable cars in various sizes and applications ran in twenty-eight American cities and in Australia, England, France, Scotland, Portugal and New Zealand. Hallidie collected royalties and sold wire rope around the world and had the energy and leisure to pursue his passions for technical education and libraries, including always his beloved Mechanics' Institute.

A GRANDIOSE WAREHOUSE
FOR THE BIGGEST FAIR YET

THREE YEARS INTO THE DECADE, the American economy collapsed. Stock markets tumbled. Panic selling, business failures and bankruptcies put thousands of people out of work, and scandals rocked the administration of the popular Ulysses S. Grant. In San Francisco, where the worst effects of the depression had already been evident for several years, the Mechanics' Institute, still preaching the glories of industrial development, pushed ahead with plans for its ninth and most ambitious industrial fair.

President Andrew Hallidie, whose prestige and influence in the city had grown with his cable car railroad, went around town, asking for support from banks, insurance firms, utilities and manufacturers. He started, as was customary and prudent, with William C. Ralston of the Bank of California. As Hallidie remembered it, Ralston said at once:

THE FIFTH PAVILION. David Farquharson, at the peak of his career as the city's leading designer of stately banks, courthouses and office blocks, was commissioned to design a new showplace for the Mechanics' Institute Industrial Fair of 1874. His "pavilion" added no luster to his reputation, but it was built to last. After seven years on its original site, the entire building was moved to a new, more prominent location at Grove and Larkin Streets, directly across the street from City Hall.

"It's a good thing for the city. Go ahead. I will stand by you." But, later, when Hallidie asked for $5000, Ralston whistled and said that was "pretty steep." He would subscribe $2500 and ask his colleague William Sharon, the notoriously tight-fisted president of the bank, to match his pledge. As usual, Sharon balked, but Ralston, after thinking it over, said: "Damn it! It's no use making two bites of a cherry. Give me that book."

With Ralston's written pledge of $5000, Hallidie was able to corral $52,530 in a few days. Several of the directors of the Institute added loans of $20,000 for a total of $106,330.60—far more than the Institute had ever raised before. As for the site, Hallidie struck a deal with a sympathetic landlord, Andrew McGreery, who offered two 100-vara lots (the old Spanish land measurements used in that part of San Francisco) on Eighth Street at Mission, in the unfashionable South of Market, for a period of five years at a rent of $1 a year, plus payment of his current (and accumulated?) taxes and assessments.

The new "pavilion," an enormous wooden warehouse with no pretensions to style or beauty, occupied almost half an acre. The area for exhibits and visitors was more than nine times that of the Mechanics' first industrial fair eighteen years earlier. There was space for hundreds of displays, including booths dedicated to famous authors (Shakespeare, Tennyson, Scott, Dickens), a bandstand, an art gallery, three fountains, innumerable flags and banners, and broad corridors for eight or ten thousand visitors at a time. Every hour or so the crowd was invited to a concert of Verdi, Weber, or von Suppé, a swirl of costumed dancers or a display of tableaux vivants. Out back was a garden, where ladies and gentlemen and their children could sit or walk or simply catch their breath, sheltered by a large tent from the stiff Pacific breeze.

ANOTHER OPENING, ANOTHER SHOW

Three thousand visitors—including all the city officials, trustees, bankers and other eminences who could be crowded onto the speakers' platform—were on hand at 11 A.M. for the grand opening of the Ninth Mechanics' Institute Industrial Fair. The orchestra warmed the air with the grand march from Wagner's opera *Tannhäuser* and the overture to Rossini's *William Tell.* The inaugural speaker was none other than Colonel (later General) William H. L. Barnes of the California National Guard, the former president of the Mercantile Library and author of that organization's hugely successful but morally compromising "Gift Concerts" at the old Mechanics' Pavilion on Union Square. Colonel Barnes was a celebrated and self-conscious orator, acquainted with juries and the moods of crowds. He paused, waiting for a lull. The *Alta California*, the city's most staid and self-important newspaper, reported:

> *The address was listened to with great attention by those who were fortunate enough to get within earshot of the speakers' stand, and closed amidst loud applause. The speaker labored under a great many disadvantages. Those who could not get near the platform were constantly walking around on the floor and in the galleries and creating considerable disturbances. Besides, there is no human voice of sufficient volume to fill that immense building—even a part of it.*

Colonel Barnes yielded the air to the three-hundred-voice blended choirs of San Francisco and Oakland, singing that all-standing rouser of every major public gathering, the "Hallelujah Chorus" from Handel's *Messiah.* "It could be heard some distance off outside the building," the *Alta* reported.

Like his now-famous predecessor Mark Twain, the reporter from the *Alta* closely studied the behavior of "young ladies," always fit subjects of journalism:

> *The most desirable and pleasant seats in the Pavilion are those placed around the three fountains in the center of the hall, and this fact was at once discovered, as the number of fascinating young ladies who occupied them will testify. The center fountain is forty-two feet in diameter and throws a stream of cool sparkling water seventy-seven feet high into the air. The smaller fountains are near the ends of the main hall, and throw spray jets which glisten in the light like diamond drops.*

Before the doors closed that evening, seven thousand visitors had paid 50 cents to get inside—or bought a season ticket for $3 (or, even better, paid just $5 for a *pair* of season tickets for a gentleman and lady). In forty-one days of August and September, the fair grossed $84,000—far more than any previous exhibition. But the cost of constructing the hall ($77,000), fitting out the interior ($29,000) and running the show ($28,000) left the management with a $70,000 debt. The only way out: another big fair next year.

A HOTBED OF FUTURE CLASSICS

THE MECHANICS' Indus-trial Fair was no Louvre, but since the first exhibition in 1857, it had become the largest, most publicized and best patronized venue for the display of original paintings, drawings, photographs and sculptures in the Far West. At the very first fair, Charles Nahl, the pre-eminent painter of gold rush scenes, and his younger half-brother, Arthur, showed their early drawings, and Eadweard Muybridge (as he was later to be known) entered several litho-graphs. At later fairs, Italian-born Pietro Mezzara, the undisputed mas-ter sculptor in California, took gold medals with his classic marble carv-ings. At the 1860 Fair, one of Charles Nahl's appren-tices, thirteen-year-old Charles Dorman Robinson, won a diploma for "the best specimen of marine drawing in the juvenile department" (Robinson matured into a highly respected marine painter).

By 1874, the art show had become a major attraction of the Mechanics' Fair. The new gallery had as much floor space as the entire exposition of 1857 and occupied most of the second story of the huge new pavilion on Mission Street. Mezzara was curator of the show, and the entries were screened by the San Francisco Art Association, most of whose members entered works in the competition. The Association had been founded a few years earlier at a meeting at the Mechanics' Institute, and for sev-eral years the Mechanics' Fair was its principal showplace. Among the entrants were William Hahn, William Keith, Thomas Hill, Norton Bush, Samuel Marsden Brookes, the Nahl brothers and Virgil Williams—the cream of California landscape painters of the nineteenth century.

THE LONE VISITOR to the gallery is likely the photographer Muybridge himself. Like the movie director Alfred Hitchcock, he enjoyed making a sly appearance in his own pictures.

MUYBRIDGE sits on a bench in this stereo view of the art gallery at Woodward's Gardens, a promenade styled after Copenhagen's famous Tivoli. Woodward's one-block park at 14th and Valencia Streets offered the paying public a small zoo, a lake, a hedge maze, an aquarium and a one-room museum of "Old Masters," skillfully copied in the 1860s by a struggling young artist named Virgil Williams, who later became an influential teacher and director at the San Francisco Art Institute—and an inspired painter of California landscapes.

YEARS OF HOPE AND DESPAIR
AS THE EASY MONEY ENDS

*W*hile our brethren in the East have been suffering from stagnation in business and want of confidence in new enterprises, we in California have moved steadily on, unaffected by the depression of the times, but with perfect confidence in the substantial prosperity of our own western home.... The Mechanics' Institute will continue to encourage young men and women to enter shops and learn trades, so that in early life, industrious habits may be inculcated and an unfailing capital [of skills and talent] be furnished, not subject to the fluctuations of the money market.

—Andrew S. Hallidie in his annual address as president of the Mechanics' Institute, 1875

1875 Mayor James Otis, twice president of the chamber of commerce, twice member of the board of supervisors and twice president of the Mercantile Library, dies in office.

1876 The Mechanics' Institute postpones this year's industrial fair to concentrate on designing the California exhibit at the Centennial Exposition in Philadelphia.

1876 The Southern Pacific Railroad opens its long-awaited connection between San Francisco and Los Angeles.

1877 Eadweard Muybridge exhibits at the Mechanics' Fair his innovative stop-motion photographs of Governor Leland Stanford's horse Occident, trotting at 36 feet per second.

JITTERY INVESTORS, frightened by the collapsing value of mining shares, rushed to withdraw their money from the Bank of California in August, 1875. The bank's cashier and proto-capitalist William C. Ralston, investor, speculator and profiteer in countless local enterprises, turned over the remains of his fortune to save the bank and walked to the Bay for an afternoon swim, from which he never returned. Architectural details in this famous drawing from *Leslie's Illustrated Weekly* are accurate. The crowd is the work of an adept engraver in New York.

1877 A staggering rate of unemployment, especially among Irish-born workmen, causes resentment that boils over in sandlot political rallies where the problem is blamed on competition from Chinese immigrants. Swayed by the oratory of the agitator Denis Kearney, rioters attack homes, businesses and employers of Chinese labor.

1878 The Workingmen's Party, spawned in San Francisco's anti-Chinese political rallies, takes control of California, imposing its anti-foreign bias on city and state governments.

THE JUDGES at the 1877 Mechanics' Fair called Muybridge's horse series "a wonderful production."

TWO PROSPEROUS "MECHANICS"
LEAD THE INSTITUTE AND THE CITY

P. B. CORNWALL

Irving Murray Scott and Pierre Barlow Cornwall were exactly the type of mechanics that the working-class founders of the Mechanics' Institute hoped to create and longed to become: inventors, employers, owners of industry. By their own success and their conspicuous wealth, Scott and Cornwall seemed to demonstrate how far a smart workman could go with good schooling, hard work and a bit of luck.

Scott was general manager of the Union Iron Works, the city's oldest and most prosperous industry and largest employer. Born in Maryland in 1837, he had studied engineering at the Mechanics' Institute of Baltimore and took his first job as a draftsman at a foundry. At twenty-one he came to San Francisco looking for work and was hired by the Donahue brothers as a draftsman at their iron works on First Street. For a few profitable years, he slipped away to the Nevada silver mines, where he designed and built machinery used in pumping, milling, reducing and refining quartz. Back at Union Iron, he rose to chief engineer, partner and manager of a shipyard that became the leading contract builder of naval vessels on the Pacific Coast.

After three years as president of the Mechanics' (1879–80) Scott formed a personal link between the Institute and the business community. The launching of each new warship engineered by Scott was celebrated with a huge reception for the workers at the Mechanics' Pavilion.

Cornwall, who was president of the Institute for eight years (1880–88), was an adventurous capitalist with interests in coal mining, real estate and electric power. He had migrated to California from Ohio before the gold rush, made his living as a merchant and participated in the state's constitutional convention and first legislature. After California's gold fever faded, Cornwall put his energy and money into such enterprises as the Black Diamond Mines in northeastern Contra Costa County, the Bellingham Bay Coal Mining Company in Washington, and the San Francisco–based California Light & Electricity Company, a primitive utility that started in 1879 (months before Thomas Edison's first company) with two dynamos and twenty-one street lamps, and grew into a part of the Pacific Gas and Electric Company.

Cornwall was in his late fifties, rich and respected, when he took on the presidency of the Institute. He brought to the Mechanics' a sharp eye for real estate value, and it was he who negotiated the purchase of the land at Larkin and Hayes Streets to which the Mechanics' Pavilion was moved in 1882.

IRVING M. SCOTT

In a critical economic history aptly titled *Imperial San Francisco*, Gray Brechin, a geographer at the University of California, Berkeley, portrays Scott and his brother, Henry, as lead players in San Francisco's obsessive drive to economically and politically dominate not only northern California but the whole Pacific Basin.

At the height of his public life in the late 1890s, when the United States seized an excuse to attack the enfeebled Spanish empire and take possession of the last of its loosely held colonies, Scott became a roaring imperialist, the like of the jingo New York newspaper publishers Joseph Pulitzer and William Randolph Hearst.

But Scott's motive as a public patriot was not merely to entice federal money to his shipyard. He sought to bolster the industrial base of a city poor in natural resources, short of capital and isolated by thousands of miles from the populous areas of the country. The shipyards that Scott promoted in the Potrero thrived into the twentieth century, producing navy cruisers, battleships and smaller vessels that were, for a time, the sum of American influence in the Pacific. Unlike the Eastern and foreign bankers who had traditionally financed the exploitation of the mineral and agricultural resources of the American West, Scott lived where he worked. He generously bought the work of local artists, headed the board of the Art Association and shared his collection with the public at the great Mechanics' Fairs. He joined his friend Andrew Hallidie in establishing the San Francisco Public Library. As president of the Mechanics' he was a regent of the University of California, and he later became a trustee of the new Stanford University.

SAN FRANCISCO GETS
A PUBLIC LIBRARY WITH A BOOST
FROM THE MECHANICS'

AFTER ELEVEN YEARS as president of the Mechanics' Institute, regent of the University of California and genius of the cable car, Andrew S. Hallidie directed his apparently boundless energy to a new task—the creation of the first free public library in California. Hallidie's usual faith in the soothing and uplifting power of popular education had recently been reinforced by a series of visits he had made, as head of the Mechanics' Institute, to a dozen other cities in the East and Midwest.

Stirred with admiration for such great free libraries as he found in Boston, St. Louis and Worcester, Massachusetts, Hallidie later told the city's board of supervisors:

> *I cannot but feel humiliated that San Francisco should have so long stood alone, not only without a great public library, but without any of those public galleries and halls which tend so much to make a community better in thought and action. [The public libraries] are the guide, the friend, the solace of the working man and toiling woman . . . and to impede their success, their progress, or their usefulness by ever so little an obstacle is a crime before God and man.*

Hallidie discovered that there was strong support for a public library among the many San Franciscans who were not obsessed by sandlot politics—and even among a few of those who were. He addressed a pro-library gathering at Dashaway Hall (the local headquarters of the national temperance and women's suffrage movements), called and chaired by State Senator George H. Rogers, a peripatetic former assemblyman from the Mother Lode who now represented San Francisco in the upper house of the legislature. In the audience were such disparate allies as the writer Henry George, who offered editorial support; a former mayor, Dr. George Hewston, who

SAN FRANCISCO'S FIRST PUBLIC LIBRARY, full of books and readers in 1881, occupied one upstairs room on the north side of Bush Street just west of Kearny. Bookshelves reached from floor to ceiling, and women, dressed up in hats and gloves, were segregated into a fenced corner.

offered books; and the radical agitator Denis Kearney, who pledged $5 of his own money to the cause.

Under California's constitution, the approval of the state government was required to enable a chartered municipality to create a tax-supported library. Senator Rogers sponsored a bill that would empower San Francisco (and other California municipalities) to levy a small property tax to build and run public libraries. Rogers took the precaution of naming himself the chairman of an honorary board of trustees to see that the city carried out its responsibility, and he packed the board with the most influential men he could enlist. They included Hallidie and his close friend Irving M. Scott, who was general manager of the city's largest industry, the Union Iron Works— and also currently president of the Mechanics' Institute. The others were Andrew J. Moulder, a former state superintendent of public instruction; John S. Hager, a former U.S. senator; E. D. Sawyer, a retired judge; Robert S. Tobin, the secretary of the Hibernia Savings & Loan; Louis Sloss, a founding partner in the Alaska Commercial Company, the great fur trade and shipping monopoly of the North Pacific; John H. Wise, a lawyer; C. C. Terrill, a contractor; and, in the odd position of treasurer, the social critic and would-be tax reformer Henry George.

Senator Rogers's bill passed the legislature without much opposition late in 1877 and was signed by Governor William Irwin the following March. Under its authorization, many California towns immediately started their own public libraries.

San Francisco alone was recalcitrant. The board of supervisors, under pressure from the city's taxpayers, balked at collecting a modest levy for a library. It was left to the honorary trustees to find and rent temporary quarters and buy books. Unpaid and unassisted, they went ahead and spent about $14,000 of their own money, hired a librarian and set a date to open the library to the public, ready or not.

The opening ceremonies on June 7, 1879, in a single, long, sparsely furnished room on the second floor of a performance hall in the heart of the theater district, lacked the bravado of most dedicatory occasions. Hallidie, with his usual eloquence, deplored the stinginess of a city government that was stalling in reimbursing the paltry sum the trustees had spent. Senator Rogers, obviously disappointed and probably also embarrassed, said: "In this condition of affairs we have thrown this room open to the public. We have not books enough to allow of their being taken out of this hall, but here you can have them as much as you please, and as soon as we can get enough to permit, they can be taken to your homes."

All day, people came in and looked at the books they could not take out.

"Though it opened under a cloud, the library was an instant success," Peter Booth Wiley has written in *A Free Library in This City* (1996):

Within days the tables in the reading room were so full that patrons had difficulty finding seats. New tables had to be bought, and often a line of would-be patrons was seen stretching along Bush Street. Within a few years, the single reading room was jammed with patrons, and employees were forced to receive and catalogue books on the tables and floor of the same room.

Faced with such competition, the Mechanics' Institute—wide-open and low-priced—continued to thrive as a members' club. Dues remained low, primarily because the Institute had been freed of debt by the success of its industrial fairs and graced with its first substantial gift, a $10,000 bequest from James Lick. Hundreds of members and nonmembers attended the Institute's classes in applied mathematics, mechanical drawing and wood and metal work, and there were waiting lists for the free lectures. The Chess Club began to attract national and international champions to matches and demonstrations that were reported like ball games in the daily papers. The book collection had grown to almost thirty thousand volumes. Many were reference works and technical manuals that were expensive and unavailable in ordinary libraries. The Institute's largest and most valuable acquisition—a complete set of the 3300-volume *Patent Reports of Great Britain*, secured for San Francisco by Andrew Hallidie had recently been sandwiched into the stacks to the delight and despair of the librarian, Horace Wilson.

"The shelves are all full," Mr. Wilson wrote in one of his annual reports to the trustees, "and many of them have two rows of books, while the closets and lockers are crowded, and many valuable works are stowed away in the basement."

Like most librarians, however, Mr. Wilson was less concerned, year after year, with the acquisition of books than their disappearance.

"There is no apparent remedy for these evils under our library system," he told the trustees in one of his many annual reports. (Mr. Wilson was librarian for seventeen years.)

It is, however, encouraging to note that these depredators have occasional spasms of conscience. Recently several valuable books, missing for years, have surreptitiously re-appeared on the shelves; while some missing folded maps were returned anonymously as "found among the effects of a deceased person," and once "conscience money" was sent to the librarian by mail.

Over at the Mercantile Association's elegant little headquarters, a few blocks down Bush Street from the new public library, the competition cut quick and deep. Paid memberships, virtually its only income, had fallen to the lowest level since its founding.

CALIFORNIA STREET, looking west from Sansome Street in 1878.

THE GRAY CITY OF THE 1880s
LOUD, WINDY AND EXPENSIVE

As seen by Robert Louis Stevenson, Scottish-born novelist and temporary Californian, in *San Francisco, a Modern Cosmopolis*:

In this camp of gold-seekers, speech is loud and the hand is ready. There are rough quarters where it is dangerous o'nights; cellars of public entertainment which the wary pleasure-seeker chooses to avoid. Concealed weapons are unlawful, but the law is continually broken. One editor [Charles de Young of the Chronicle] was shot dead while I was there; another walked the streets accompanied by a bravo, *his guardian angel. I have been quietly eating a dish of oysters in the restaurant, where, not more than ten minutes after I had left, shots were exchanged and took effect; and one night, about ten o'clock, I saw a man standing watchfully at a street corner with a long Smith-and-Wesson glittering in his hand behind his back. Somebody had done something he should not, and was being looked for with a vengeance. It is odd, too, that the seat of the last vigilance committee I know of—a mediaeval* Fehmgericht *[secret tribunal]—was none other than the Palace Hotel, the world's greatest* caravanserai, *served by lifts and lit with electricity; where, in the great glazed courtyard, a band nightly discourses music from a grove of palms. So do extremes meet in this city of contrasts; extremes of wealth and poverty, apathy and excitement, the conveniences of civilization, and the red justice of Judge Lynch.*

As seen by Caroline H. Dall, feminist, philosopher and Proper Bostonian, in *My First Holiday* (1881):

At risk of repetition, I must try and draw a picture of this strange city. No one who has never seen it can imagine its bleak aspect. Imagine a three-pointed rock rising from an ocean, hid in black and envious fogs. Across these summits, lifted by almost perpendicular ascents, the intersecting streets strike like huge steps, by which they must be climbed. If I look down when half way up the hill, or if I look across from the upper windows of the Palace Hotel, I seem to see a city built of stone.... No green thing flaunts the air. The houses crowd upon one another.... A few dismal-looking trees of stone color, with their branches tied down, may be seen. Down in the close streets the atmosphere is like that of other large cities; but climb to the crest of a hill, where you can catch the full force of the trade-wind, and it seems to stop your very breath.

... After lunch we went to the Mechanics' Fair in the Mission Street building. On the lower floor we had the usual exhibition of manufactures and inventions.... There were, of course, superb minerals. A great many things were exhibited cut from a shell called Abalone, or Venus's Ear. The lovely colors and shades of the shell are skillfully adapted—but these articles are very expensive; for which there is no excuse that I know, except that the polishing is done by hand. Three dozen buttons would have cost me thirty-six dollars! And I saw nothing pretty under ten or fifteen.

OLD SCORES, NEW INVENTIONS AND SIGNS OF BETTER TIMES

1880 Lester Allen Pelton takes out a patent on a water wheel with buckets like pairs of spoons. In the years ahead, the Pelton Wheel, manufactured in San Francisco, becomes a world standard for hydroelectric generation.

1881 Milton Kalloch, eldest son of Mayor Isaac "Sorrel Stallion" Kalloch, is found not guilty (self-defense) of murdering Charles de Young, the gun-slinging, libel-printing editor-publisher of the *San Francisco Chronicle*. Eight months earlier, de Young had ambushed, shot and wounded the elder Kalloch. This causes some San Franciscans to suspect that Milton was after revenge. The decision surprises Milton's lawyer so much that he swallows his chewing tobacco.

1882 Congress passes—and President Chester A. Arthur signs—a law suspending for ten years the right of Chinese to immigrate to the United States. The first Chinese Exclusion Act is extended periodically for thirty-five years, then supplanted by more general restrictions.

1883 The late James Lick, who grew rich as a miller and real estate developer, leaves the Institute $10,000 for the purchase of technical and scientific books.

1884 Adelina Patti, the leading European soprano, makes her San Francisco debut in *La Traviata*, *Rigoletto*, *Lucia*

SAN FRANCISCO'S FAVORITE BOULEVARDIER, Joshua Norton, self-proclaimed Emperor of the United States and Defender of Mexico, died in 1882, aged sixty-two.

IN THE LOBBY OF THE INSTITUTE, a bronze plaque that survived the fire of 1906 commemorates the generosity of James Lick.

di Lammermoor and other Italian operas at the Grand Opera House on Mission Street.

1885 The Coast Seamen's Union, predecessor to the Sailors' Union of the Pacific, organizes to fight wage cuts by West Coast ship owners.

1886 On San Francisco's first Arbor Day (inspired by the poet Joaquin Miller and funded by the millionaire mining engineer Adolph Sutro), schoolchildren plant hundreds of eucalyptus trees on Yerba Buena Island.

1886 A few adventurous men, attracted by reports of gold on the Forty Mile River in the Yukon Territory, leave San Francisco for the long sea voyage to St. Michael, just below the Arctic Circle, ten years before richer discoveries in the Klondike.

1887 San Francisco is blanketed in early February with a rare and heavy snow.

1887 Ambrose G. "Almighty God" Bierce, the savage polemicist and literary dictator of the Pacific Coast, moves his mordant pen to the *San Francisco Examiner*, recently acquired by the young William Randolph Hearst.

1888 The United States establishes a quarantine station on Angel Island, later enlarged (1909) to an immigrant station ("the Ellis Island of the West Coast") for arrivals from the Pacific.

THE MECHANICS MOVE UP IN THE CITY AND THE WORLD

IN RECENT YEARS, the official opening of every Mechanics' Industrial Fair (we are now at number seventeen) has consisted of a long afternoon of orchestral overtures, poetry, prayers and oratory in some acoustically suitable auditorium like the Metropolitan Temple or the Grand Opera House, capped off with a living tableau of adult, white, male mechanics, dressed in leather aprons, jeans, heavy boots, goggles and helmets and armed with the ham-mers, wrenches, saws, rivet guns and other tools of their trades.

In the new Mechanics' Pavilion at Civic Center, the formalities start out the same in August, 1882. They begin with the praying and the poetry at 2 o'clock of a Tuesday afternoon and drag on until it is almost time to open the doors to the public at 7. But the tableau vivant of machinists in work clothes has disappeared from the program. As a

DISMANTLED AND MOVED, BOARD BY BOARD, one city block from 8th and Mission Streets to the block bounded by Larkin, Grove, Polk and Hayes Streets, the drafty old Mechanics' Pavilion became a drafty new Mechanics' Pavilion, right across the street from the unfinished City Hall. The Institute paid the owner of the "sandlots"—the Roman Catholic Archdiocese of San Francisco—$175,000 in cash for the derelict property, a one-time cemetery that recently had become a nuisance and embarrassment, the staging ground for anti-Chinese demonstrations and other political mischief. To pay for the site, the trustees of the Institute put up $5000 of their own money, took $5000 from the treasury and mortgaged the library building on Post Street for $165,000. The architectural firm of Curtell & Eisen designed a re-use plan, and the weather-worn building was treated to an imposing new Baroque façade, designed by the original architect, David Farquharson.

CONSTRUCTION OF THE "NEW" CITY HALL began in 1872, lasted twenty-seven years and cost $6 million, a towering sum that was scattered among numerous contractors, many of whom apparently overcharged or used substandard materials. When the skinny dome collapsed in the first seconds of the great earthquake in April, 1906, the good citizens of the badly governed city said they always knew the whole thing was corrupt. The Mechanics' Pavilion (upper left, with flag flying) survived the quake but succumbed to fire a few hours later.

INSIDE THE GREAT HALL, the exposition remained gaudily, delightfully the same with its popcorn and soda pop, its colored streamers and topiary shrubs, its webs of wire rope and bales of cotton, its fountain for trysting and its art galley, as always, for social climbing.

result, perhaps, of the costly and risky decision to dismantle the tacky old building, dress it up with faux granite and Italianate window frames and rebuild it next to City Hall, the mechanics have arrived at a new definition of themselves and of their position in society.

A mechanic is no longer to be depicted as a man in greasy overalls and oily boots, working with small hand-tools in a smoky shed. A mechanic is a technician, an inventor, a manufacturer, a rich, creative, politically active industrialist like the current leaders of the Institute—Irving M. Scott, P. B. Cornwall or Andrew Hallidie.

For years, Hallidie has been hounding the city's capitalists to quit speculating in mining claims and real estate and put their money into industrial development. "One man who starts a successful manufacturing enterprise is of more value to the community than ten men who invest their all in savings banks, to loan on real estate," Hallidie says. An educated and ambitious mechanic, in Hallidie's view, matures into a manufacturer, an inventor, an employer.

The welcoming address is delivered by an eminent Napa County banker, lawyer, district attorney, legislator and collector of internal revenue named Chancellor Hartson. Judge Hartson, according to the *Evening Bulletin*, succeeds in covering "all phases and uses of the mechanic arts through all ages of the world since the Creation." He enumerates—and elaborates upon—the marvelous works attributable to the "mechanics" of the current century: the steamboat, the locomotive, the telegraph, the telephone, the electric light, the cable car.

"As the Parthenon added largely to the luster and renown of Athens," Judge Hartson concludes, "so the Mechanics' Institute will contribute to the just fame of San Francisco through coming ages, down to the last syllable of recorded time."

Few others have compared the Mechanics' Institute with the Parthenon, or suggested that the cluster of unfinished public buildings on the sandy western edge of the small city of San Francisco resembled the Acropolis of Athens. But the size, the trimmings and the location of the new Pavilion all signify that the humble mechanic has reached his destiny as a leader of the city.

OF CHESS AND CHESSMEN AND MEN AND WOMEN WHO PLAY CHESS

CHESS IS AN ANCIENT and difficult game requiring concentrated intelligence and spatial visualization. The contest is usually limited to two competitors (or a small team, pooling brains), scowling silently over a small, checkerboard table. Rarely does it involve betting, drinking, body contact, noisy crowds or sex. In short, chess is not the sort of recreation generally associated with the early years of San Francisco as an American city. Yet the playing of chess and the seclusion to make it possible were essentials of both the Mercantile and the Mechanics' libraries from the day of their creation in the grab-and-run social scene of the gold rush.

Perhaps it was the intellectual and fraternal qualities of chess that attracted young men to the quiet chess rooms of the two membership libraries. San Francisco was a lonely place, full of strangers on the make from around the world, and most of its seductive entertainments—its saloons, casinos, dance halls and brothels—were costly, dangerous and degrading. The Chess Room, like the library, gave a man a place to get off the street, meet some friends and possibly even improve his mind.

As the city grew and settled down, the stimulating and competitive atmosphere of the pioneer chess rooms—especially that of the Mechanics' Institute—attracted young professionals, businessmen, doctors and lawyers. In the 1880s, the game gained increasing attention and prestige in Europe and North America. Famous chess players from abroad toured the United States, visiting local clubs and demonstrating their brilliance in blindfold, multi-board matches and exhibitions with severe time limits, conceded pawns and other handicaps.

The first world-class player to visit the thirty-year-old Mechanics' club was Johannes Hermann Zukertort, a German resident of England, who stormed San Francisco in 1884, a year after he had won a game from the reigning champion, Wilhelm Steinitz. Claiming for the moment to rank number one in the world, Zukertort took on such local heroes as the young lawyer Joseph D. Redding in matches at the Mechanics' Institute, the Mercantile Library and Redding's home base at the Bohemian Club. It is recorded that he may have lost a game or two to the best of the Mechanics' club.

By then, it seemed obvious that the Mechanics' Chess Club had earned its private space, its special status in an educational institution dedicated to the "mechanic arts." As to whether chess was, indeed, a "mechanic art," a sedentary sport or merely a demanding mental exercise, argument remained.

As international grandmaster Siegbert Tarrasch wrote in *The Game of Chess*:

Chess is a form of intellectual productiveness. Therein lies its peculiar charm. Intellectual productiveness is one of the greatest joys—if not the greatest one—of human existence. It is not everyone who can write a play, or build a bridge, or even make a good joke. But in chess everyone can, everyone must, be intellectually productive and so can share in this select delight.

JOHANNES ZUKERTORT held onto his unofficial "championship" only until 1886, when Wilhelm Steinitz defeated him in a famous match in New York City. Steinitz retained his world leadership against many challengers until 1894, when he lost to Emanuel Lasker. Zukertort died at forty-five of a brain hemorrhage following an intense game in London in 1888.

THE CHESS ROOM GOES ON LINE

Inspired by a recent chess match on an international cable connection between a team in London and a team in New York, a chess club in Victoria, British Columbia, challenged San Francisco to a long-distance match on a telegraph connection to be supplied free of charge by the Canadian Pacific Railroad. The Canadians had recently enrolled several strong players from England, and they clearly expected to catch the overbearing American city by surprise.

The Mechanics' Chess Club, headed by Walter R. Lovegrove, a twenty-five-year-old amateur who had been playing chess since childhood, accepted the challenge and agreed to a two-game match on the night of May 31–June 1, 1895. At each end of the wire would be two chess boards and two teams of consulting players. Both boards would be in play at the same time. In theory, each move would have a ten-minute limit, although the process of transmitting the data might (and did) slow the game.

A few years earlier, Dr. Lovegrove, a dentist by profession, had beaten the putative champion of California, Joseph Redding, a lawyer and the chief musical librettist of the Bohemian Club. Dr. Lovegrove maintained his local and state leadership for decades to come. His reputation for concentrated and ruthless play, plus the known talent of his teammates, gave the San Franciscans confidence that they could master a group of unknown players from an island up north. The *San Francisco Chronicle* speculated ahead of the event that the Mechanics' club would "strike terror into the heart of the north by some brilliant combination beyond the scope of the ordinary mortal, but within the reach of genius."

Play began on both boards at 6:30 Friday evening, and the match lasted until 7:15 Saturday morning. Victoria took one game and lost the other. Thomas Piper, the English-born captain of the Canadian group, blamed the lost game on some missing players and a lack of time for preparation; but the Canadian chess historian Stephen Wright, after a detailed study of the celebrated match, decided it was "sheer fatigue" that did them in.

Two weeks later, the Mechanics' club defeated Vancouver, British Columbia, two games to zero, in a similar telegraph match. Both Redding and Lovegrove, the top players in California, were on the winning side. The San Franciscans dispatched a taunting telegram to Victoria, proposing a rematch.

"You ought never to let it remain a tie," they wrote. "Either be the star club or else surrender. Lovegrove says he would like to have another whack at [Thomas] Piper, but will have to wait till Victoria has trained up for the Stars of the West."

Piper responded with ironic exaggeration that his club would be a faint light among such dazzling stars as San Francisco. He suggested settling all grudges with a three-board competition that fall, but, for one reason or another, the two clubs never fought it out again. Years later, when the Mechanics' Chess Club again scheduled telegraphic matches, it was with more traditional rivals, the chess champions of Southern California.

A DIFFICULT (NOT IMPOSSIBLE) STRATEGY TO WIN

James J. Dolan, secretary and sometime president of the Mechanics' club in the early years of the twentieth century, challenged his fellow players to analyze the strategy for White to win a remarkable chess position. Dolan's study perplexed the best analysts in the club and proved so challenging that it was printed in books and magazines around the world. C. E. C. Tattersall, in his then-famous text *A Thousand Endgames* (1911), called it "the most difficult study in the whole of this collection."

Robert E. Burger, a veteran member of the Mechanics' club, writes in his book *The Chess of Bobby*

Fischer (1975): "The legendary San Francisco master Dr. W. R. Lovegrove, who had just defeated the touring Harry Nelson Pillsbury in an exhibition match, was the first to produce a complete solution [to Dolan's study]. The *Literary Digest* picked it up in 1904 as a promotional competition; only one correct solution was entered. The notoriety of the study was such that around the world it was familiarly referred to as 'The San Francisco Endgame.'"

The solution, according to Burger, involves several Zugzwangs, forced moves.

A DECADE OF HIGH HOPES AND BITTER DISILLUSION

1890   The Mechanics' Institute starts the decade optimistically. In ten years, membership has grown from around 1500 to more than 4000. In the same period, net worth—including the library, the Pavilion and other real estate—has grown from about $225,000 to more than $1.3 million. President David Kerr urges the trustees to enlarge the library and Chess Room, and add a lecture hall, laboratory and more classrooms. In the ensuing depression years, little of that gets done.

1891   Stanford University enrolls its first class (including one future president, young Herbert Hoover of Iowa), on the former stock farm of Senator and Mrs. Leland Stanford at Mayfield, near Palo Alto.

1891   President Benjamin "Little Ben" Harrison pays a midterm visit to the West Coast, looks at naval yards, checks the progress of vessels under construction and makes friends with West Coast shipbuilders.

1892   The Sierra Club is founded, with John Muir as its first president.

1893   A national economic depression hammers business in the Bay Area, leading to wide unemployment. Just before Christmas, the Union Iron Works sponsors a reception at the Mechanics' Pavilion at the Civic Center for workers and managers (including the chief engineer Irving M. Scott, former president of the Institute) to celebrate the completion of the cruiser USS *Olympia*. With such

THE SAN FRANCISCO ART ASSOCIATION, founded twenty-two years earlier at the Mechanics' Institute, acquired the forty-room Victorian mansion of the late Mark Hopkins, one of the "Big Four" financiers of the Central Pacific Railroad, and turned it into a teaching center and showplace for students and professionals in 1893. The mansion was destroyed by the 1906 fire. In 1926, its aerie at the crest of Nob Hill became the site of the Mark Hopkins Hotel.

government contracts, Union Iron is able to employ 1300 men and boys.

1894   The Mechanics' Institute, postponing its own industrial fair to next year, participates in planning, building and supervising the California Midwinter Exposition in Golden Gate Park. Irving M. Scott, a former president of the Institute, works closely with the chairman, the newspaper publisher Michael H. de Young, raising money, signing up exhibitors and transporting exhibits from the World's Columbian Exposition in Chicago.

YEAR-OLD STANFORD UNIVERSITY and the University of California played their first "Big Game" (90 minutes long) in a field at Haight and Stanyan Streets in San Francisco in 1892. Stanford's manager, Herbert Hoover, forgot to bring a football from Palo Alto, but Stanford won anyway, 14 to 10. This photo in 1900—same sport, same schools, same playing field—shows little improvement in equipment or venue.

CALIFORNIA MIDWINTER FAIR

January 27–July 4, 1894

THEY PROMISED an "international" exposition, and, sure enough, fifteen foreign nations sent displays from the World's Fair in Chicago to the five-month run of a much smaller show in distant California. The Midwinter Fair invaded Golden Gate Park over the protests of the strong-minded park director, John McLaren. Contractors graded the sand dunes and built a "Sunset City" of domes and minarets and carnival rides. Four large temporary buildings—Moorish, Egyptian, Mogul and Old Spanish Mission–style—faced inward around a plaza. At the center was the *clou*, as architects call it—the tower that would become a symbol of the exposition.

The Midway (its name, like most of its concessions, came fresh from the Chicago Fair) provided a Hawaiian Volcano in occasional eruption; a hootchy-kootchy dance by Little Egypt (one of several authentic incarnations of the Chicago original); and Daniel Boone's Wild Animal Show, with performing pigs, acrobatic goats and a nasty lion named Parnell, which killed its keeper early in the run of the show. At the center rose the Firth Wheel, a locally designed version of Chicago's famous Ferris Wheel, which was rather too big to move west.

In all, it was a small, tacked-together event, not much more than an expanded Mechanics' Fair with the Midway added. Still, it pleased the ambitious, self-conscious city and created some jobs in construction, maintenance, food service and tear-down. To what extent it fulfilled the financial and promotional expectations of Michael de Young, Irving M. Scott and the other city fathers who had put up $40,000 in seed money, is impossible to measure. Unlike most expositions before or since, the Midwinter showed some measure of profit—around $32,000 over its $2 million cost. Times were tough in the nineties, and the freeze on jobs and money persisted everywhere.

More than a century later, the Music Concourse, two wild-eyed granite sphinxes, the Japanese Tea Garden and a frequently remodeled and rebuilt art museum named for de Young are the only visible remains in the park. Hardly anyone knows how, when or why they got started.

THE 272-FOOT BONET "ELECTRIC TOWER," a miniature descendant of the Tour Eiffel of Paris, twinkled with more than three thousand lightbulbs, installed by their manufacturer, General Electric. From the top beamed a shaft of colored light, usually aimed at the Stonehenge-like Sweeney Observatory atop nearby Strawberry Hill.

SURVIVING THE GRAY NINETIES

IN HIS ANNUAL ADDRESS to the Mechanics' Institute early in 1895, the usually optimistic Andrew Hallidie declared that he had never witnessed such a bad period as the "disastrous" year just past.

"California has felt the oppression," he said, "and San Francisco has not, to my recollection, suffered so much since the Fraser River gold mining excitement" [1858].

In the face of national depression, the Mechanics' Institute had boldly scheduled its Industrial Fair in January and February instead of the usual time in late summer. The result was a social and financial fiasco. The Institute lost more than $2000, which it could ill afford, and the notion got around that industrial fairs had had their day. To make matters worse, someone had come up with a scheme to require everyone who bought a season ticket to become a member of the Institute. As a result, 1400 new members signed up for a year and then dropped out. The librarian, Horace Wilson, called this massive defection conclusive proof that there was no gain in forcing anyone to join a library he didn't want to use.

In many respects, however, the Institute thrived during those lean years. An enrollment of 122 young men and women (of whom about a hundred regularly attended class) signed up for courses in crayon work, industrial design, geometrical drawing, machine drawing, architectural drawing and electrical science. Membership in the Library slowly increased. The Chess Room hosted championship matches and took on foreign competition by telegraph. In the very year that Hallidie called "disastrous" for the nation, the Institute spent a fifth of its yearly budget on repairing and remodeling the library. "I believe the dark clouds are rolling by," Hallidie said, "and that we have already obtained glimpses of the silver lining."

Hallidie remained a passionate advocate of technical education. He saw a positive trend, an extension of the historic role of the Mechanics' Institute, in the founding in 1888 of Cogswell Polytechnic School by the wealthy, teetotaling dentist Dr. H. D. Cogswell, and in the later establishment of technical high schools with bequests from the Lick and the Wilmerding estates. Although the bad year 1895 was Hallidie's last as president of the Institute, he remained a regent of the University of California, by gubernatorial appointment, until his death from heart failure in 1900, at age sixty-five. The University's continued use of the Institute as a San Francisco campus for mechanical arts reflected Hallidie's political and philosophical influence.

Ernst A. Denicke, the German-born banker who followed Hallidie as president in the second half of the decade, guided the Institute through a period of uncertainty and gloom into one of growing self-confidence. In the venturesome spirit of the late 1890s, Denicke urged the Institute to build a magnificent new library on the site of the thirty-year-old building on Post Street.

"Our library is handy for ladies coming down town shopping, and for business men desiring to take books home," Denicke said. "It is adjacent to every car system, and can be reached for one fare from every part of the city." He had only sympathy for "our friends"—the Mercantile Library—who had moved several years before to new quarters at Van Ness and Golden Gate Avenues, out of the vibrant downtown district.

Aside from location, however, there was little in the headquarters building for the comfort and convenience of patrons. "During the last three lectures," Denicke complained, "the hall was overcrowded in a degree dangerous to life and limb, and in spite of the crowding it was impossible for all to hear."

To miss a lecture at the Mechanics' in those days was to miss the latest scholarship on Confucianism, socialism, or prehistoric archaeology; on Egyptian art, the Kimberly diamond mines or the history and religion of Syria. Admittedly, Professor Eugene Hilgard's findings on the irrigation systems and drinking water of California were pretty technical, but who could fail to be fascinated, listening to the eminent biologist David Starr Jordan, the recently appointed president of the new Leland Stanford University? Dr. Jordan's topic was "Evolution: What It Is and What It Is Not."

NEW SCHOOLS, NEW BOOKS AND TOO MANY BIKES

1894 The California School of Mechanical Arts (today's Lick-Wilmerding High School) is founded with a $540,000 bequest from James Lick "to educate males and females in the practical arts of life." The Lick School later merges with a school founded in 1900 with the bequest of J. C. Wilmerding, who specified that his money be used "to teach boys trades fitting them to make a living with their hands with little study and plenty of work."

1895 A craze for tandem bicycles infects young and old, especially those who can't handle the tricky new one-wheelers. The *Argonaut Weekly* urges the city to license bikes. "Unregulated, they are becoming a dangerous nuisance."

1896 Sutro Baths, a vast indoor swimming pool with an upstairs museum of mummies, music boxes and tropical plants, opens on a cliff at Land's End.

1896 Ships of the Alaska Commercial Company, returning from the Far North, bring samples of gold to San Francisco from the Klondike River in Canada's Yukon Territory, setting off the last great gold rush in North America.

1896 Irving M. Scott, former president of the Institute and chief engineer of Union Iron Works, invites more than a thousand workers and managers to a reception at the Mechanics' Pavilion to celebrate their construction of the battleship *Oregon*.

1897 The Mechanics' Library installs its first public telephone for members' use. "From the harvest of nickels gathered by the company, it would seem to be much appreciated," the librarian reports.

1897 Banker William Crocker, the son of the railroad builder Charles Crocker, and William's brother-in-law, Andre Poniatowski, develop a hydroelectric system on the Mokelumne River, later part of the Pacific Gas & Electric Company.

1898 On February 15, a boiler room explosion sinks the USS *Maine* on a "courtesy call" to Havana.

1899 Frank Norris's novel *McTeague*, about the moral disintegration and gruesome death of a brutish San Francisco dentist, encounters critical praise and expressions of outrage.

JACK LONDON, self-educated in the libraries of Oakland and San Francisco, published his first short stories, many based on his recent experiences in the gold rush, in *Overland*, San Francisco's literary monthly.

THE HUNTINGTON SISTERS—Alyce Esther and Stella—checked out books at the Mechanics' Library one afternoon in the late 1890s. The librarian, who frequently complained about the discomfort and "extreme shabbiness" of the old place, was proud of the library's "liberal and prompt supply" of the latest publications.

OPENING OF THE MINING FAIR
AND CLOSING OF THE JUBILEE.

TO STIR UP EXCITEMENT for the opening ceremonies of the Mining Fair, the *San Francisco Call* published an artist's concept of President William McKinley touching a telegraph key in Washington to get things started at the Mechanics' Pavilion.

IN THE EXPANSIVE MOOD of the late 1890s, the Mechanics' Institute attempted one too many industrial fairs in their great Pavilion at the Civic Center. The first was the Thirtieth Mechanics' Fair, held in late summer 1897; the second a Mining Fair put on the following winter by the California Miners' Association with the support of the Institute. The Mining Fair was to be the climactic event in a celebration of fifty years of gold production in California.

Although the most recent Mechanics' Fair had closed with a $5000 profit for the library, it made money only by offering enticements that, in the words of President Ernst Denicke, sometimes "smacked of the fakir." The Institute was forced to sponsor games, contests and cheap entertainments that left a bitter taste in Denicke's mouth. He had reason to hope that a five-week display of San Francisco–made mining machinery and precious minerals in February and March, 1898, would be clean, wholesome and profitable.

The Golden Jubilee began on January 24, 1898, the fiftieth anniversary of James Marshall's find at Sutter's mill. Mostly, it consisted of parades, banquets, band music and oratory. For days ahead, the newspapers published nostalgic memoirs of the gold rush and special editions illustrated with drawings of bearded miners wearing slouch hats. Although the self-styled Forty-Niners were actually a small

and vanishing minority in San Francisco, ordinary citizens were urged to honor them as the spiritual founders of the city. In the opening-day parade up Market Street there was a full lineup of alleged pioneers, wearing golden sashes across their chests, and imaginary pioneers in recently purchased red flannel shirts, denim Levis and leather boots. The Mechanics' Institute entered a float that looked like a giant mining cart, overloaded with gilded rocks and festooned with banners advertising the forthcoming Mining Fair. Baritones, sopranos and student choirs sang hymns at the Native Sons' Hall and other appropriate places, and there were widespread readings of such verses as "The Days of Gold, the Days of Old, the Days of Forty-Nine." At night, the city shot off fireworks from three of its most accessible heights: Nob Hill at Clay and Jones Streets, Noe Hill at 21st and Sanchez Streets and Rincon Hill at the southeast bay front.

During the Jubilee, nobody in San Francisco at first paid much attention to newspaper stories reporting that the battleship *Maine* had just arrived in Havana to pay a "courtesy call" on Cuba, where the Spanish had been harshly and unsuccessfully trying for several years to suppress an independence movement. At the end of the week, the California Miners' Association opened their five-week Mining Fair in the Pavilion at Larkin and Grove Streets.

President William McKinley stood by at the White House to touch a telegraph key that would signal the opening. An afternoon of poetry and speeches ensued before the ordinary folk were let inside at 7 o'clock.

One might have thought that all Californians, self-conscious, boastful, intoxicated with glorious memories of the gold rush, would have flocked to see the latest products and machines of the mining industry. In truth, most Californians apparently had lost interest in mining—especially gold mining—since the ruling of U.S. Circuit Judge Lorenzo Sawyer in 1884 that effectively outlawed the hydraulic extraction of gold from the ravaged foothills of the Sierra. Hydraulic mining and deep quartz mining, in any case, had never been romantic—not like crouching down and finger-picking nuggets out of the sand in places with names like Dry Bones, Hangtown and Poverty Gulch. As for honoring the Forty-Niners as founders of the city, everybody knew that very few of the city's real founders and current leaders had made their pile by wielding a pick or shovel.

Right in the middle of February came another, serious distraction. The *Maine* exploded and sank in Havana harbor, and the United States went to war against Spain. Suddenly, the piles of ore and glass cases filled with record-breaking nuggets seemed irrelevant. San Franciscans set their minds instead to "Remember the Maine."

The Mining Fair lost so much money that its sponsors could not scrape up the rent they owed the Institute. They offered to leave in place seven hundred Welsbach gas mantle lamps, worth a dollar or two apiece, that they had strung up to light the show, and some heavy draperies they had used as sound barriers. The Institute accepted the lamps and drapes as the best part of a bad deal. The Welsbach lamps, a recent invention of the German metallurgist Carl Auer von Welsbach, burned a mixture of air and gas to heat a mantle to incandescence, and they were cheaper to operate than conventional gaslights. It was said they were being used as streetlights in many progressive towns in Europe. For several years, they lighted the vastness of the Pavilion.

President Denicke, always a gentleman, blamed

THE RECTANGULAR DISPLAY of granite cones and arching banners advertising the chief products of Tuolumne County bore a strange resemblance to a river barge, loaded with ore and carrying a single, lonely passenger through the vast and echoing spaces of the Mechanics' Pavilion. Several of the new Welsbach lights gleamed overhead like upside-down lampposts. Neither the minerals nor the display of up-to-date mining machinery attracted the throngs of jabbering schoolchildren and young women who were usually the most enthusiastic visitors at Mechanics' Industrial Fairs.

the failure of the Mining Fair on the times rather than the boring exhibits and the unpopular theme. He was glad, he said, of the service the Institute had been able to provide to the community and to the mining industry. He admitted to being skeptical about the future of industrial expositions in general.

"Time was," Denicke said in his address to the annual meeting, "when the Mechanics' Fair was looked forward to as the one event of the year… a great social function for which everybody was waiting and to which everybody went. All this has changed. The City has grown rapidly in every way, and amusements, both good and cheap, have multiplied greatly. So the Exposition of our manufactures and productions, even with the added charm of a promenade concert, has ceased to be the drawing card it was a few years ago."

He recommended that the annual industrial exhibition be held only once every three years. The interval might give "an air of novelty" to the famous old show.

THE LAST INDUSTRIAL FAIR—1899
Welcoming the new Colonials

EXCITED BY VISIONS of an American empire in the Pacific—with its capital, of course, in San Francisco—the Mechanics' Institute decided to put on another industrial exposition (the thirty-first) without waiting to let the public forget several recent, relatively dismal fairs. This would be a larger, more worldly exposition—a *Colonial Exposition*.

The Philippine Islands, which seemed closer and more important to San Franciscans than did Cuba, would be the centerpiece, surrounded by exhibits from the Pacific Coast of Asia, "from Vladivostock to Singapore," the Hawaiian Islands and all the nations, states and provinces on the Pacific side of North, South and Central America. Congress had refused to consider a $50,000 appropriation to underwrite the Colonial Exposition; but the trustees of the Mechanics' Institute were convinced that the time was ripe for San Francisco to assert its leadership in Pacific commerce, even without federal support. The war was winding down, or so it seemed. The California Regiment of volunteers was returning in triumph from Manila. The papers were carrying articles about the products of the Philippines and the beauty of the native people of the islands.

This would be an exhibit of people more than products. The principal task would be to gather human specimens of various skin colors to represent the great diversity of America's Pacific empire. P. J. Healy, a trustee of the Institute, enrolled a family of Yokut Indians from Mendocino County, and Joseph Cumming, the board's secretary, supervised the construction of appropriate tule huts where the Yokuts could weave baskets and make arrows. The War Department pledged free transportation from the Islands for nineteen Filipino villagers and an assortment of representative products.

The *San Francisco Bulletin* headlined a story in advance of the opening: "Red Men Join the Filipinos: The Newest and the Oldest Americans Shake Hands at Mechanics' Pavilion." By opening night, according to the *Bulletin*, the Pavilion would contain "representatives of nearly every white race on earth" and several nonwhite ones. These exotic specimens would be showing their handicrafts in Filipino cottages, Indian wigwams, Japanese and Chinese tea gardens, Hawaiian huts, an American log cabin, Grecian temples and a small Eiffel Tower.

Along with the Filipino villagers, the Army sent a full troupe of circus performers. President Ernst Denicke, hiding his dismay, told the first-night crowd: "[The circus] will enable you to form an idea of the physical status of this strange people, and later on when our industries and our schools have found a firm footing we will no doubt be able to show you much more of the everyday life of this one of Uncle Sam's new possessions."

Mayor James Phelan advised the audience: "As you watch the little band of Filipinos trip about through this building, remember that they must not be regarded as the spoils of war so much as the representatives of the new fields which have been gathered together under the protective care of the American Nation...."

Mayor Phelan's speech, in the words of the *Bulletin*, "fairly bristled with the spirit of patriotism, and, although delivered in the midst of confusion and the noise of machinery, was frequently applauded."

When the receipts and bills were added up, the Thirty-First Industrial Exposition showed a loss of $7600. Whether the loss was caused by the added cost of feeding and housing the Filipino circus was hard to say. The Mechanics' had meant to do another fair the following year, 1900. But the fighting dragged on in the southern Philippines, and young men were charging off to Alaska every summer to hunt for gold. The trustees decided to let the Mechanics' fairs die with a whimper instead of a bang. In coming years, they would rent the Pavilion for other less troublesome, more profitable shows.

INTIMATIONS OF THE FUTURE
AND CELEBRATIONS OF THE PAST

1900 A man dies in Chinatown of a disease identified by scientists as rodent-borne bubonic plague. City and state officials and most of the newspapers scoff at the threat of an epidemic. Nine years later, after 280 confirmed cases, 172 deaths and the extermination of thousands of infected rats, the plague dies out.

1901 Seven thousand boxing fans pay $2 to $20 to see heavyweight champion Jim Jeffries brush off challenger Gus Ruhlin in five rounds at the Mechanics' Pavilion.

1902 On Independence Day, President Theodore Roosevelt announces that the war against the insurgent Filipinos is officially over.

1903 Orville and Wilbur Wright fly a manned, controlled, power-driven, heavier-than-air craft more than 800 feet over the Atlantic Dunes at Kitty Hawk, North Carolina.

1904 Amadeo Peter ("A. P.") Giannini launches the Bank of Italy—later to become the Bank of America—primarily as a source of loans to small business owners in the wholesale produce district.

1905 The first cable connection between San Francisco and Hawaii opens for business.

1906 San Francisco's Olympic Athletic Club hosts the A.A.U. American Amateur Boxing Championships at the Mechanics' Pavilion (April 4, 5 and 6).

THE MECHANICS' MONUMENT at Market, Battery and Bush Streets was dedicated to the mechanics of the city by its donor, James Mervyn Donahue, who commissioned Douglas Tilden to sculpt the group of muscular artisans as a memorial to his father, Peter Donahue, an Irish-born blacksmith. The bronze figures, on an imposing pedestal by Willis Polk, were exposed in all their nakedness on May 14, 1901, with appropriate oratory by Mayor James Phelan, filling in for President William McKinley, whose heavy schedule of banquets, receptions and dedications in the Bay Area had been curtailed by the illness of his wife. Phelan reminded the crowd that the small machine shop started by Peter Donahue and his brother had grown into Union Iron Works, the city's largest and most important industry. Later in the week, President McKinley showed up at the Union Iron shipyard to launch the battleship *Ohio*, named for his home state. Four months later, McKinley was dead, assassinated at the World's Fair in Buffalo by a more than slightly crazy anarchist named Leon Czolgosz, who was executed six weeks later for his crime.

DR. H. NELSON JACKSON, a physician from Vermont, and his chauffeur, Sewell K. Crocker, in a brand-new Winton auto car, make the first transcontinental automobile crossing from San Francisco to New York in seventy days (May 23 to August 1, 1903). A few weeks later, E. T. "Tommy" Fetch, a demonstration chauffeur at the Packard agency in San Francisco, and Marius C. Karrup, the editor of an auto magazine, make the trip in a Model F Packard, besting the Jackson-Crocker record by nineteen days, but too late to share the glory.

THE LAST YEARS OF THE GREAT PAVILION

There always was something going on at the Pavilion, something public, wholesome, physical and large. Whenever a president came to the city—"Little Ben" Harrison, Bill McKinley, Teddy Roosevelt—he spoke to as many thousands as could be packed inside. Whenever a boxing title came up for grabs the rivals duked it out under the blazing arc lights. Athletes of the Olympic Club competed in a "Circus Olympiad" in the style of ancient Greece in 1893, three years before the first games of the modern Olympiad. Dwight Moody preached salvation to wayward souls, and his gospel singer Ira Sankey sang hymns that brought on hysterical tears and mass conversions. Adelina Patti, the coloratura soprano, raised her small, clear voice to the rafters, and Pietro Mascagni, renowned for his operas, conducted a great Tchaikovsky symphony. There were Irish dances, ballroom dances, cakewalk dances, and, now and then, a huge memorial service.

On the last night before the hall burned down, roller skaters wearing masks and carnival costumes competed for prizes offered by a downtown department store. The winners never collected because the department store, like the Pavilion, was gone the next day, April 18, 1906.

THE GREAT HALL OF THE FAR WEST. For twenty-three years, flags flew every day (sometimes at half-mast) above the mansard corner towers and peekaboo gables of the Mechanics' Pavilion at Larkin, Grove, Hayes and Polk Streets. Hammered together in 1874, dismantled and moved to the Civic Center in 1882, frequently painted, decorated and remodeled, the aging Pavilion was notable primarily for its size. Boosters claimed it was the largest building in the United States. The trustees of the Mechanics' Institute pondered what to do with it—and, more importantly, with its valuable site.

WILLIAM MCKINLEY had been more popular in San Francisco than any other president since Lincoln. His death by an assassin's bullet moved the city to a massive show of affection and grief. Ten thousand mourners were admitted to the Mechanics' Pavilion on September 19, 1901, while thousands stood outside, straining to hear the eulogy by Mayor James Phelan and the chorus and orchestra performing McKinley's favorite hymns. Black-and-white banners and swathes of dark green cypress draped the balconies, and an immense canopy of purple and white flowers spelled out the president's last words—barely legible at the end of the hall: "Goodbye all. It is God's way. His will, not ours, be done."

"FITZ"　　　"TOM"

WYATT EARP, whose mythic role as a fast-draw marshal in frontier Arizona was currently under construction in the dime novels of Ned Buntling and on the pages of the *San Francisco Examiner*, was living quietly with his wife, Josephine, in the respectable, middle-class Richmond District when he was hired to referee one of the most controversial boxing matches ever seen at the Mechanics' Pavilion—the encounter between heavyweight champion Bob Fitzsimmons and challenger Tom Sharkey on December 2, 1896. Earp's presence attracted more attention than the preliminary bouts, and he delighted the crowd by wearing a holster packed with a Colt six-gun, of which he was publicly relieved by a police captain. Earp made a lot of enemies in the eighth round by calling a foul on Fitzsimmons and giving the win to Sharkey, who had been losing for seven rounds. The *San Francisco Call*, sensing that Earp's illegal pistol was a publicity stunt contrived by the hated *Examiner* (where Earp had been working as a bodyguard to the editor), mocked Earp's pretensions with a cartoon that showed him literally armed to the teeth and handing the $10,000 purse to "Tom" (Sharkey). Earp paid a $50 fine for toting a hidden weapon. It is not recorded what he made as referee, nor whether the *Examiner* reimbursed him for the fine.

JAMES J. CORBETT lost a tough one to the heavyweight champion James J. Jeffries in the tenth round of their title match in the Mechanics' Pavilion on the night of August 14, 1903. "Gentleman Jim," as the sportswriters called him (although Corbett disliked the nickname), was the most popular boxer the city ever produced, a real home-town, Irish-American kid who had trained at the Olympic Club and worked his way up to Club champion, Golden Gloves champion and boxing trainer before he turned professional at age twenty-three. He took the world heavyweight title from Boston's favorite, John J. Sullivan, in 1892 and lost it after five years to Bob "Ruby Robert" Fitzsimmons, who lost it to Jeffries. Corbett was trying a comeback that night at the Mechanics'. Most of the ten thousand spectators—"the largest crowd ever assembled at ringside in this country," the *New York Times* reported—were backing "Gentleman Jim." But Corbett's fine and fancy footwork was not enough to avoid Jeffries's fists. In the tenth: "Jeffries sent a left hook to the stomach and Corbett went down for nine seconds. He got up and received a left to the stomach and a right on the jaw. He went down, and after the count of seven Tommy Ryan threw up the sponge. Corbett was suffering pain and a chair was brought for him. After a minute's rest he recovered and got up and shook hands with Jeffries."

THE CHESS ROOM WELCOMES
(and sometimes wallops)
THE CHAMPS OF THE WORLD

Two chess players fighting over the board may fitly be compared to two famous generals encountering each other on the battlefield, the strategy and the tactics being not dissimilar in spirit.

— British chess writer Alain C. White,
in the *Encyclopaedia Brittanica*, 1929

B Y THE BEGINNING of the twentieth century, the Mechanics' Chess Club had gained an international reputation as one of the strongest regional clubs in North America. It also could claim to be one of the oldest clubs in the United States, tracing its origins back to a corner table in the one-room Mechanics' Library in 1855, just a few years after the first-ever international chess championship in London in 1851.

Foreign champions, visiting San Francisco on world tours, scheduled demonstrations at the Institute in which they would take on as many as a dozen or more challengers in simultaneous games. German-born Emanuel Lasker, the reigning world champion, faced thirteen opponents on eleven boards at the Mechanics' one afternoon in 1902. Lasker had taken the leading position in the world of chess from the brilliant Wilhelm Steinitz in 1894, when Steinitz was approaching sixty and Lasker was twenty-five, and the young strategist was still in top form.

To the delight of the San Franciscans, the unshakable Lasker was beaten by a three-man consultation team of local amateurs and was compelled to resign in a game with Nathaniel J. Manson, the then-president of the Mechanics' club. A few days later, the Mechanics' most brilliant amateur and frequent champion, Walter R. Lovegrove, upset Lasker in a match that lasted four hours.

An occasional defeat was not unknown to such master professionals as Lasker, but the victory of Dr. Lovegrove, a thirty-three-year-old dentist, was pure joy for all the chess players of San Francisco. Lovegrove's skill became the substance of legends, and his sixty-year association with the Mechanics' attracted other top players to the upstairs Chess Room at the Institute.

Lasker, the greatest tactician of his era, held his title for twenty-six years against the strongest opponents in the world, including even Steinitz in a celebrated rematch. He lost at last to the Cuban José Raúl Capablanca in 1921.

EMANUEL LASKER (1868–1941) was among the five original grandmasters of chess by proclamation of Czar Nicholas II of Russia in 1914. Of the five (Lasker, Alekhine, Capablanca, Marshall and Tarrasch), all but Siegbert Tarrasch, a brilliant strategist and teacher who never became world champion, played at the Mechanics' Chess Room in the twentieth century. In the last decades of his life, Lasker wrote several books on chess, won prizes as a pigeon breeder and became a friend of Albert Einstein, who called him "one of the most interesting people I came to know in my later life."

THE WASTED GENIUS
OF AMERICA'S BEST

Harry Nelson Pillsbury was, by all accounts, the strongest professional chess player the United States had ever produced. That he visited the Mechanics' Chess Room for a few days in 1904 was precious recognition of the high standing of the San Francisco club. That he was beaten there by a brilliant amateur in a game he could not analyze was even more significant.

Pillsbury had undertaken to show his virtuosity by playing sixteen games of chess blindfolded, plus four games of checkers and six hands of whist. The show-off performance was Pillsbury at his best: he won every game except two of chess. One loss was to Dr. Walter R. Lovegrove, the Mechanics' top player and frequent state champion for the past twenty years, the other to a three-man consultation team of members of the San Francisco club.

Lovegrove's game so puzzled Pillsbury that he spent most of the night analyzing the moves. The following morning, Lovegrove won again. Pillsbury analyzed that afternoon, and Lovegrove again overcame the champion's analysis. Already debilitated by an untreatable, fatal disease (from which he would die two years later at age thirty-four), Pillsbury had achieved a lasting place in chess history by his incredible powers of concentration. A few years before his embarrassment at the Mechanics' club, he had demonstrated this unique gift by memorizing a random list of words put together by an English surgeon and a civil engineer, who thought to trip him up with the hermeneutic vocabulary of biochemistry and obscure geographic references to the recent Boer War in South Africa. Pillsbury studied the list for a few minutes, put it aside and recited it, backward and forward. Next day, without peeking at the list, he did it again.

HARRY NELSON PILLSBURY

Bill Wall, an American chess historian, has tracked down the meaning of most of the obscure and technical words on the devastating list: *antiphlogistine* (a medication against inflammation); *periosteum* (a membrane sheathing a bone); *takadiastase* (an artificial food); *plasmon* (a form of cytoplasm); *ambrosia* (the food of the gods); *Threlkeld* (the name of the skeptical surgeon); *streptococcus, staphylococcus, micrococcus* (three strains of bacteria); *plasmodium* (a fungus); *Mississippi* (if you can spell it, you've got it); *Freiheit* (German for freedom); *Philadelphia; Cincinnati; athletics; no war* (no problem); *Etchenberg* (a coined word? or somebody's name?); *American; Russian; philosophy* (another disarmingly easy series); *Piet Potgieter's Rost* (Potgietersrust, a town in South Africa); *salamagundi* (a stew); *Oomisillecootsi* (a Zulu general); *Bangmanvate* (a place in Zimbabwe); *Schlechter's Nek* (site of a British engagement with Boer rebels); *Manzinyama* (a lake in South Africa); *theosophy* (a spiritual doctrine); *catechism* (a classic exercise in memorization); and *Madjesoomalops* (a concoction of pickles and herring, presumably popular in South Africa at the time).

Although this demonstration did not occur at the Mechanics' Institute, Pillsbury earned a fond place in the club's history by playing and losing to the local hero.

THE DECLINE
AND FALL OF
THE MERCANTILE

THE FATAL ILLNESS of the Mercantile Library, which once called itself, with justifiable pride, "the principal library on the Pacific Coast," began at its moment of greatest success. In 1870, the proceeds of a $500,000 "gift concert" lottery and two smaller lotteries freed the Mercantile of debt for the first time in several years and brought its existence (and its chronic lack of money) to the attention of thousands of people who had never heard of it. At the same time, the fund-raiser compromised the reputation of the Mercantile as an institution of social and intellectual distinction.

The Mercantile achieved its moment of solvency just as the city and the nation were falling into business stagnation and financial chaos. The run on the Bank of California in 1875 and the sudden and mysterious death of its chief executive, William Ralston, knocked out the Mercantile Library's most reliable

THE MERCANTILE LIBRARY'S beautiful building on Bush Street (1868) was included by Carleton E. Watkins in his stereo views of San Francisco's landmarks.

source of support. Other paying subscribers began to seek better uses for their money—and dues were about the only income the library had.

By 1878, the Mercantile again was running out of cash and found it shamefully necessary to put on another series of fund-raising "gift concerts." As before, the Mechanics' Institute provided a venue, this time in its Eighth and Mission Pavilion, a massive shed with the acoustics of a livestock pen and space for five thousand seats on the main floor and five thousand in the gallery. For $2 a ticket, or $5 for the three-concert series, ordinary folk were offered a chance to win a prize "of great value" and also to hear a raise-the-rafters musical program by a 200-member orchestra and a 2000-person chorus, climaxing in the "Anvil Chorus" from Verdi's *Il Trovatore*, with "electricity used to fire the artillery." The public response was disappointing. At the end of the year, the Mercantile was left with $531 in cash and $350 in unpaid bills. Membership was the lowest since the founding of the library in 1853.

The opening of the San Francisco Public Library in 1879 further drained the patronage of the Mercantile. Two blocks up the street from the Mercantile, the new public library offered the same sort of books, and it was free. Men's and women's clubs, business associations, fraternal orders, colleges and universities began to command the allegiance—and the dues—that had once belonged to the Mercantile. Disheartened members petitioned their leaders to merge the library with the Mechanics' Institute.

The Mercantile's ability to maintain its independence for another twenty-six years, despite dissension, corruption, bad judgment and financial starvation, was due only to the stubborn determination of a few individuals to keep it alive. Soon after the lovely new building at 216 Bush Street was built and paid for, the leadership of the Mercantile concluded it was inadequate, badly located and expensive to run. As early as 1876, just six years after the first great lottery, the board of directors came up with a plan to sell the building for $250,000, buy a lot in another downtown location for $55,000, build a larger, cheaper structure and save the difference, which they figured would give them $100,000 to run on. At a poorly attended meeting of members, the plan was voted down.

"From that time on," said Edward Gray Stetson, who was president in 1881, "we may date the decline

THE LADIES' READING ROOM of the Mercantile Library, photographed in the 1870s by Eadweard Muybridge, was nationally famous for its likeness to some fashionable sitting rooms on Nob Hill.

of the Mercantile Library." Stetson inherited a treasury with $4.23 in the bank and $250 in unpaid bills.

Throughout the generally prosperous 1880s, the income of the library relentlessly declined. The librarian took a salary cut, the main lecture hall was leased to the Academy of Sciences and most of the street floor was rented to retail shops. Dues were lowered, but membership continued to fall.

In January, 1887, President A. A. Wilkins reported: "Nothing of interest has occurred to vary the monotony of the preceding ten years." The membership had fallen from more than 2000 to 896. The directors borrowed $3000 at 6 percent to stay afloat. The next year, they borrowed another $3500. By the end of the decade the debt would reach $9000, and there would be only about 400 paying members.

In January, 1889, a spark of hope was ignited by the installation of a new president, Eusebius J. Molera, an architect and civil engineer in his early forties. Molera had energy and connections: he belonged to a handful of clubs, was married to a niece of General Mariano Vallejo, had an international reputation as a designer and builder of lighthouses, was willing to remain president for five years—and was determined to solve the housing problem.

The board offered the Bush Street headquarters at auction, but there were no bidders. Another year of indecision and disappointment passed before a real estate deal came together. Pacific Telephone & Telegraph Company bought 216 Bush Street and let the library stay there temporarily for $500 a month, while the Mercantile bought a lot at the southeast corner of Van Ness Avenue and Golden Gate, hired outstanding architects (Pissis & Moore) and planned a five-story edifice of stone, brick and terra cotta.

Nothing went right. For lack of money, the Mercantile had to settle for a smaller, cheaper building made of reinforced brick with terra cotta trim. Pacific Telephone & Telegraph raised the monthly rent at Bush Street to an unsustainable $750. The librarian was fired for embezzling $1300.

The grand opening of the new building on February 6, 1892, occasioned a concert, a postcard solicitation for new members and the establishment of a Whist Club to liven up the empty space. Membership was up by 25 percent from the nadir.

An auxiliary was formed, three women joined the board and membership briefly soared, only to tumble again. Amid national economic depression, the upstairs rental space stood vacant. Members urged the board to move the library downtown.

Plagued by debt, complaints about the location and continued lack of revenue, the directors considered renting the building as a hotel and moving the library again—or, as an alternative, melding the library into the Public Library or the University of California. The new location was clearly a bad mistake. The directors hired as librarian the poet Ina D. Coolbrith, but eight more agonizing years of fund appeals, guest lectures, membership drives and charity balls would not lift the Mercantile off its downward course.

On January 2, 1906, after years of loose discussion and months of close negotiation, the Mechanics' Institute agreed to accept all members of the Mercantile Library Association as life members and to consolidate the two institutions for a period of fifty years. The libraries would be combined as the "Mechanics'-Mercantile Library."

Within a few months of the consolidation, all of the two hundred thousand volumes, accumulated, protected and fought over for fifty years, would be totally destroyed.

SHATTERED EARTH AND FLYING FIRE

THE GREAT EARTHQUAKE of April 18, 1906, lasted 48 seconds. The fires that started in broken gas pipes lasted four days. The loss of 3000 lives and millions of dollars in property lasted forever.

On that terrible morning, hotels collapsed and sidewalks twisted and buildings burned to the ground while broken mains oozed water that could not reach the fires. People stood in the streets in numb silence and watched the fires and wondered whether the terrifying aftershocks were warnings of Armageddon. Nobody knew what was happening to the city or to the rest of the world—only what his eyes could see. Every survivor had his own view, a glimpse of the incomprehensible reality.

"I was awakened by the house creaking and shaking and pitching so rapidly that I fell out of bed in trying to arise," one man recalled. "I jumped up, grabbed an overcoat and ran through the hall, being thrown against the walls a couple of times before I reached the street. My wife, with a blanket thrown around her, had got there ahead of me. The earth seemed to be in a great convulsion, and the street was full of small fissures, luckily none of them very large. Chimneys and brick walls were falling everywhere, killing many people. A man was killed in the same house I occupy by a brick chimney falling from across the way through his bedroom window."

No one was in the three-story building of the Mechanics' Institute on Post Street when the earth moved. It was 5:13 in the morning. The great Mechanics' Pavilion at the Civic Center was empty, too, locked and silent after the last of the roller skaters had gone home.

In the strange silence that followed the quake, the janitor of the Pavilion, M. G. Buckley, walked around and saw that the huge, wood-frame building was standing more or less intact, despite its age and the great length of its roof beams. Across Larkin Street, the masonry dome of City Hall had crumbled, and the Central Emergency Hospital at street level had collapsed into rubble.

As Buckley remembered it, the first victim of the earthquake brought to Central Emergency in a horse-drawn vehicle was the critically injured fire chief, Dennis T. Sullivan, who had been buried in falling bricks and scalded with steam from a burst radiator. Seeing that there was no assistance at the ruined hospital, the driver of the carriage was turning away when Buckley threw open a side door of the Pavilion and offered shelter. A doctor and nurses who had been rescued from the wreckage by a policeman from City Hall Station rushed across the street and began moving their patients into the Pavilion. In less than an hour an emergency facility was in operation, and wagons and carriages were bringing in hundreds of the seriously wounded and dying.

Later in the morning a huge fire, moving eastward through the Hayes Valley, began to threaten the area, and the patients at the Pavilion had to be carted immediately to hospitals and shelters beyond the reach of fires that had erupted downtown and South of Market Street. Fire Chief Sullivan died several days later at the Southern Pacific Hospital near Golden Gate Park.

That afternoon, the "Ham-and-Eggs Fire," which had been started accidentally by a woman on Hayes Street who lit her leaky gas stove to cook breakfast, swept irresistibly into the Civic Center. First, sparks and windblown debris ignited the Mechanics' Pavilion. From there, the fire leaped over Larkin Street, gutted the shells of the battered public buildings and destroyed most of the records of the City and County of San Francisco. The fire took three days to gnaw its way through City Hall. The wooden Mechanics' Pavilion burned overnight to charcoal and ashes.

It was almost impossible during that day and the next for anyone to reach the center of the downtown district. The streets and sidewalks were blocked with rubble. Bricks and stones and chunks of concrete were falling from masonry buildings, and structures that had survived the first major quake were collapsing in the aftershocks. As the fires spread, soldiers from the Presidio were ordered to dynamite threatened buildings to curb the fires. On orders from the mayor, looters were to be shot on sight.

The Mechanics' librarian, Frederick M. Teggart, somehow found his way to Post Street soon after the quake, before the downtown fires started. One look at the ruins of 31 Post Street told him the library was doomed. Only a single wall was standing, the one bearing a bronze plaque of James Lick that the trustees had commissioned in gratitude for Lick's generosity to the Institute. The rest of the three-story building was a pile of broken masonry. Teggart went home to Berkeley on the first ferry he could find and began sending letters and telegrams to libraries, scientific and trade associations and government agencies, asking for help in replacing the lost books.

Joseph Cumming, the secretary to the board of trustees, got to the building in time to move some records out of two safes in the library into the safe deposit vault of the Crocker National Bank. He managed to save twenty-five years of board minutes, the ledger of members, some leases and contracts and

LOOKING DOWN LARKIN STREET from Golden Gate Avenue on the afternoon of April 18, dazed spectators stood alone or huddled in small groups and watched smoke from the burning Mechanics' Pavilion (hidden on the right) begin to blanket the ruined City Hall.

the original copy of the Institute's constitution, signed by the first directors. Most of the other records of half a century were down in the basement in a large brick vault. They were all destroyed.

One of the regular players at the Mechanics' Chess Room sent word to the American Chess Bulletin in New York that the Mechanics' Institute was "no more."

"It was the headquarters of all chess players here," he wrote, "in fact, the only club in the city. No doubt there will be another fine library erected on the site … but for the present chess clubs are 'non est.'"

A world champion, the Hungarian Geza Maroczy, had been scheduled to play at the Mechanics' for a week at the end of April. He cancelled his visit and went to New Orleans instead.

THE SIDE ENTRANCE to the Mechanics' Pavilion was crowded with horse-drawn carriages bringing the dead and injured to an emergency hospital that functioned there for a few hours after the quake. All the patients were moved to safety before the Pavilion caught fire that afternoon.

THE DESIRE FOR READING
(and playing chess)
BEGINS ANEW

When everyone stood in the bread lines and cooked on the street, and when candles were the only lights, no one had time to think of books; but with the resumption of normal conditions came the desire again for reading. Many members have told me that of all things they were deprived of they missed the library most.

—Joseph M. Cumming,
Secretary to the Institute, May, 1907

AT THEIR REGULAR semi-monthly meeting, on the night before the great earthquake, the trustees of the Institute had fretted, as trustees are wont to do, about the future of their properties—the old Pavilion, which scarcely paid the cost of running it, and the forty-year-old library building, which was crowded, uncomfortable and uneconomic, considering the high value of its downtown location.

Ten days later, when Joseph M. Cumming, the longtime secretary (equivalent to a staff director), finally got in touch with the president, Rudolph Taussig, the two men agreed that, as far as the future of the buildings was concerned, the problem had been solved. Both buildings were gone, and only the naked ground remained.

Few institutions in San Francisco had suffered such total loss. The building at 31 Post Street was completely destroyed—its reading rooms, its Chess Room, its classrooms and its 140,000-volume library of technology and science, including the huge (if seldom used) collection of British patents dating from the reign of James I. Gone, too, were the 60,000 books of the Mercantile Library, which had merged its exquisite collection into the Mechanics' only four months earlier. Gone was the great old Pavilion, the scene of so many boxing matches, concerts, trade

shows, commemorative festivals and presidential addresses.

In a sense, all of San Francisco had lost its past: all documents of the city government, the courts, the tax assessor, the registrar; the libraries of the Bohemian Club, the Society of California Pioneers, B'nai Brith and the San Francisco Public Library; most of Adolph Sutro's 200,000-volume personal library, including more than 4000 priceless incunabula; and, of course, the combined acquisitions of the city's two oldest educational institutions for adults, the Mechanics' and the Mercantile.

Taussig wanted to get the trustees together, and he sent Cumming around in a hired buggy to scare them up. Only seven of the fourteen could be found in San Francisco. On May 1, they came to Taussig's house on Fulton Street, west of Van Ness Avenue (known ever after as "The Street That Stopped the Fire"), wearing old clothes, flannel shirts and bathrobes. They lacked a legal quorum, but they decided to give Teggart authority to spend $5000 on books and to keep them in his home in Berkeley until the Institute had a place with shelves.

To maintain a presence in San Francisco, the seven trustees agreed to open a temporary headquarters, a simple little building on the edge of the devastated Pavilion block. On May 23 they had the shack open

TEMPORARY HEADQUARTERS of the Mechanics' Institute from May through August, 1906, was a 12-by-20-foot shed with a flat roof and one small window on a slab of concrete, surrounded by trash from the burned Pavilion. Facing Larkin Street between Grove and Hayes, it stood where carts and buggies had brought wounded victims of the earthquake to the temporary emergency hospital on the morning of April 18.

and mailed out letters to the members—as many as could be located—to tell them the new address.

A few weeks later, President Taussig sent a letter to the scattered membership to assure them that the library would be restored "as expeditiously as possible." The Institute had cash on hand, he said. With that and the insurance on the lost buildings, there should be no delay in putting up a temporary library building and buying a new collection of books.

> *In restoring the Library, your Trustees will give special attention to American, English, German and French literature (Belles-Lettres), History, Biography and Travel, maintaining in this respect the best traditions of the Mechanics' and Mercantile libraries. Also that we may bear our part in the rebuilding of the City, the fullest representation will be given to book[s] in Architecture, Engineering, Commercial and Industrial subjects.*

Members could help, Taussig suggested: "By returning all books to the Librarian at the earliest possible moment; By filling out their present address and mailing the enclosed card; By making suggestions in writing for the consideration of the New Permanent Building Committee; [and] By sending in their dues."

Later, the trustees sent out another note requesting addresses "whether changed or not since the fire" and announcing that dues for May, June, July and August [$1.50 of the $6 annual dues] would be waived. The Institute had lost track of more than one-quarter of its members who had died, dropped out or fled the city.

In August, four months after the disaster, the Mechanics' Institute and Mechanics'-Mercantile Library reopened in a temporary building at 99 Grove Street—the southeast corner of Polk and Grove, now Polk Hall of the Bill Graham Civic Auditorium. The librarian reported that 5000 books were on the shelves, and the number was growing daily. Many had come as gifts from the United States government and from such sympathetic institutions as the Alameda Public Library, the American Institute of Architects, the John Crerar Library of Chicago, the American Society for Testing Materials, The New York Public Library and The Royal Society of London, and members of the Institute contributed hundreds of books from personal collections that had escaped the fire.

THE MAKESHIFT BUILDING AT 99 GROVE STREET was inelegant and drab, but it offered a cheap and fast solution to the housing problem. Its street front was landscaped with window boxes planted with red geraniums, and a row of vines along the baseboards climbed the unpainted walls. The front door was ornamented with a rustic wooden gable, designed and built by Arthur F. Mathews in the fashionable Arts-and-Crafts style. Mathews was a longtime friend of President Taussig, who had given the Institute a large Mathews mural that was destroyed in the earthquake and fire. (Later, the Institute would commission Mathews to paint the floor-to-ceiling canvas that enriches the lobby of the Institute's building at 57 Post Street and is reproduced on page 76.) Construction limped along while the Institute was filing insurance claims. Scheduled to open near the end of June, the building finally was completed in August. By then, the cash settlements had started coming in, and the trustees turned their minds to permanent quarters.

THE TEMPORARY LIBRARY, a clean, well-lighted place, just 60 by 120 feet, offered patrons sturdy reading tables, hard wooden chairs and a private corner—not visible here—for playing chess and checkers. The walls were lined with shelves to hold the growing collection of books. The first acquisitions were dictionaries, encyclopedias, technical reference works and popular fiction. Later, the librarian began adding literature and history. Lewis R. Meade, who took over the presidency from Taussig for one year, reported in March, 1907, that the collection had grown to 17,000 volumes since the day of the earthquake and fire. Meade added, presumably in jest: "I fear very soon we shall be confronted with the ever-present problem—how to find more room."

THE "GREAT WHITE FLEET." Sixteen battleships from the U.S. Navy's Atlantic fleet, on a world voyage of friendship and intimidation, reached San Francisco from Acapulco on May 6, 1908, and received a rapturous welcome from the people of the battered city. Some 14,000 crew members and officers enjoyed themselves for two months before sailing off to Hawaii and points west on their mission to impress the world with America's soft voice and big stick.

SAN FRANCISCO TIME LINE

The recovery

SHIPS IN THE BAY
MUSIC IN THE AIR

1907 Like a discordant coda to the disastrous earthquake fires, the castle-like Cliff House, a landmark built in 1896 by Adolph Sutro, is swept away by an accidental fire.

1908 Muir Woods in Marin County becomes a national monument.

1912. About 4000 women exercised their recently won franchise to vote in a municipal election. Among them were (left to right) Miss Lucretia E. Raill, Miss A. C. Herndon and Mrs. Luisa Carter, assisted by two unidentified male precinct workers. At issue was an $8.8 million bond proposal for the new Civic Center, to include a new city hall, civic auditorium and main library. The issue passed with an astounding plurality of eleven-to-one, although only about 30 percent of those eligible bothered to vote.

1909 A festival named for Gaspar de Portolá, the Spanish commander who stumbled onto San Francisco Bay in 1769 while searching for Monterey, celebrates San Francisco's progress in recovering from the earthquake and fire.

1910 Opera diva Luisa Tetrazzini gives an outdoor concert on Christmas Eve to a crowd estimated by her sponsors (the *Chronicle*) at 250,000.

1911 The newly formed San Francisco Symphony presents its first concert, with Martha Richardson, soprano of the Paris Opera, as soloist.

1913 Congress approves and President Woodrow Wilson signs the Raker Act, giving San Francisco development rights to the waters of the Tuolumne River, including permission to dam and flood the magnificent Hetch Hetchy Valley in Yosemite National Park.

1914 Silas Christofferson, who has been ferrying passengers in a hydroplane between the ports of San Francisco and Oakland, makes the first solo flight from San Francisco to San Diego in a Curtiss biplane ... The first vessel to reach the city via the Panama Canal arrives at the Embarcadero.

WHILE LIBRARIAN Francis B. Graves was buying and begging books to fill the shelves of the reopened Mechanics'-Mercantile Library, the trustees resumed their interrupted debate on the future of the institution. They were agreed on one thing only—that there must be a new building. Where it should be was uncertain. (A few favored Union Square, where one found the better shops.) As to the size, contents, financing and design of the building, there were, as usual, diverse opinions.

Two elements were certain: First, the building should be large enough to accommodate a major, general library; and second, it should generate income from rental space to augment the limited revenue from members' dues, which were still $6

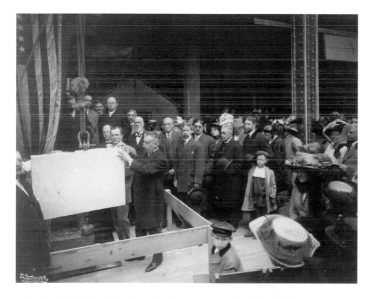

PRESIDENT RUDOLPH TAUSSIG maneuvered a slab of Tennessee marble into its corner position at the new headquarters building on September 5, 1909. The street number would now be 57 Post, but the location was exactly that of the 1866 structure at 31 Post, leveled by the earthquake and fire. The architect Albert Pissis stood among the onlookers with his derby hat against his chest.

a year. During the first months of discussion, Lewis R. Meade, who had taken over as president for 1907, blundered into a hornets' nest by suggesting that the Chess Room ought to be "abolished" to make space for profitable rentals. The outcry was so instant and so heartfelt that Rudolph Taussig was compelled to return to the presidency, utter many reassuring words, hire an architect and begin at once to plan a large building on the Post Street lot, with plenty of space for the library, plenty of space for rentals and plenty of space for chess.

To plan the building, the trustees, urged on by Taussig, chose Albert Pissis, one of the most distinguished—and certainly the most traditional—of the city's classic architects. Pissis was known for his stately structures of steel and stone. For the Mechanics' he proposed a nine-story steel-framed mixed-use building, finished in reinforced sandstone on a granite base, with a symmetrical, severely classical facade. The street floor would be rented out as retail space; the second and third floors would be library and offices. On the fourth floor there would be a room for the Chess Club, and the rest of the building would be given over to offices for rent. The cost of construction would run close to $250,000.

Rich in real estate and free of debt, the Institute pushed ahead, secured a bank loan and announced its plans to the newspapers early in 1909, just short of three years after the disaster. The general contractor, Lewis A. Hicks Company, started work in April. That fall, as the framework began to rise, the Institute invited members and friends to see the ceremonial placement of a marble cornerstone over a buried box containing current municipal reports, a telephone directory, some silver coins and a medal from the 1893 Mechanics' Fair, awarded to the first piece of native-grown-and-spun silk fabric produced in California.

RAISING THE ROOF

THE PLANS BY THE DISTINGUISHED ARCHITECT Albert Pissis were crisply classical in style. Every detail reflected Pissis's attention to classical architectural style and his wide experience in the design of public and commercial buildings. During the planning and construction of the Mechanics' building, three of Pissis's previous structures were under reconstruction in downtown San Francisco, having been gutted by fire after withstanding the earthquake: the Emporium, the Flood Building and the Hibernia Bank at Jones, McAllister and Market Streets. New and taller buildings have since risen to the right and left of the Mechanics' Institute, and the cable car running along Post Street has been replaced by a bus; but the Mechanics' has remained virtually unchanged except for occasional changes of street-floor tenants. San Francisco Architectural Heritage, in its definitive inventory of downtown buildings, *Splendid Survivors* (1979), drew attention to "the very beautiful circular iron and marble stairway" and called the building "a major San Francisco cultural landmark."

STEEL BEAMS WERE HAND-LIFTED with cable and pulleys at 57 Post Street in autumn, 1909, while "sidewalk superintendents" maintained close watch. Horse-drawn wagons delivered Albert Pissis's carefully chosen materials: metal framing cast in California; white Manti sandstone from Utah for the exterior facing; indoor woodwork of Oregon pine; Belgian black marble and Tennessee pink marble for the lobby and the walls of the circular iron stairway. By 2005, when the Institute celebrated its sesquicentennial, the building had survived ninety-five years of changing tastes, minor earthquakes and periodic revolutions in architectural style, testimony to the value of sober design, rugged materials and respectful use.

BORN IN MEXICO, ALBERT PISSIS was brought by his family to San Francisco at age six, educated here and sent as a young man to the rigidly classical Ecole des Beaux-Arts in Paris to perfect his talent for drawing. On his return to the city in 1880, he found work designing houses in the popular Eastlake, Italianate and Queen Anne styles, later lumped together under the broad term "Victorian"—or, less regally, "carpenter gothic." On his own, after a period of designing large brick warehouses and small commercial buildings, he made his mark with the Hibernia Bank (1892), the James Flood Building (1904), the Emporium (1896, rebuilt 1908) and Temple Sherith Israel (1904). In the course of these major projects, he became not only the city's best-regarded exponent of classical architecture but also its wealthiest practitioner. After the earthquake and fire, he designed the White House department store (1908—later to become a multi-use block of parking and street-level retail stores) and Lane Library (1911—now the Health Sciences Library of California Pacific Medical Center). Pissis was known for his strong opinions, self-critical honesty and stubborn insistence on controlling the selection and quality of building materials. As a member of a commission to consider rebuilding the ruined City Hall, he joined the majority in advising that it be promptly torn down, one of the less difficult decisions of the post-quake period. At the time of his death in 1914, he was one of five leading architects on a panel to select designers for the principal buildings of the 1915 Panama Pacific International Exposition.

THE JOY OF MOVING

TOWARD THE END of June, 1910, the trustees of the Institute sent a letter to the members announcing that 57 Post Street was ready for business, except for the permanent steel shelving in the library (delivery delayed by a strike). The library would open anyway, using shelves from the temporary headquarters, in mid July. Meanwhile, any member who knew of prospective tenants for the stores and offices was "earnestly requested" to give their names to the secretary. The new phone number was SUtter 829.

The building, of course, had not been paid for. For the next two years, a mortgage of more than $300,000 hung over it, draining the Mechanics' revenue for books, periodicals, lectures and classes. While the city was pondering how and where to replace the Civic Center, the Mechanics' entertained proposals from would-be purchasers of the vacant Pavilion lot, which they had bought thirty years before for $175,000 and figured now was worth a million dollars. One developer presented a scheme for a 14,350-seat auditorium, costing $400,000, to be built by the sale of stock at $1 a share. He showed a drawing of a convention center in Kansas City to give a rough idea of what he had in mind, but he did not come up with the money to buy or rent the land.

Fortunately, the voters approved $8.8 million in bonds early in 1912 to build a new Civic Center. The city offered $700,000 for the Pavilion lot; the Mechanics' gladly accepted; and the block became the site of the municipal auditorium. Originally called the Exposition Auditorium, the building was constructed by and for the 1915 Panama Pacific International Exposition. In 1999 it was renamed the Bill Graham Civic Auditorium to honor the late promoter of rock music.

The Mechanics' Institute spent about half the proceeds of the sale to pay off the mortgage and invested the rest in San Francisco municipal bonds, an arrangement that suited the city well. The newspapers printed a staged photograph of guards dragging out two big bags allegedly filled with $700,000 in currency. It was an ingenious variation on the trite picture of two smiling gentlemen passing a check from hand to hand, and it made the city look more generous than it had ever been.

THE STEEL SHELVING was in place, painted olive green to complement the woodwork of Flemish oak, when photographer R. J. Waters came to take an official picture of the third-floor reference room soon after the new library opened in the summer of 1910. Technical books, periodicals, patent records and books on the fine arts were housed on this floor; the main reading room was on the floor below.

TWO PALACES, THREE MUSES
AND A WORLD EXPOSITION

The architect Albert Pissis deliberately left an empty wall for artwork in the front hall of the new Mechanics' Building at 57 Post Street. The distraction of the 1915 Panama Pacific International Exposition, which drew heavily on the leadership of the Institute and on the talents of many local artists and architects, delayed completion of the plan until 1917, when the trustees commissioned the eminent California muralist Arthur Frank Mathews to create a floor-to-ceiling painting for the east side of the lobby.

The new wall painting was intended to replace in spirit an earlier Mathews mural that hung in the Mechanics' Library and was lost in the earthquake and fire. Similar in style and scale to Mathews's massive scenes of the history of California (1914) in the rotunda of the state capitol in Sacramento, it shows three Parnassian women ("The Arts") and a bearded, monk-like man standing by while a small crew of carpenters and masons work on an unfinished dome. The dome appears to be a direct descendant of the Church of Hagia Sophia in Constantinople, but to San Franciscans it bore a clear resemblance to Bernard Maybeck's Palace of Fine Arts at the recent Panama Pacific International Exposition, where Mathews had exhibited sixteen paintings, painted a large mural called *The Victorious Spirit* and served as a member of the international jury of awards.

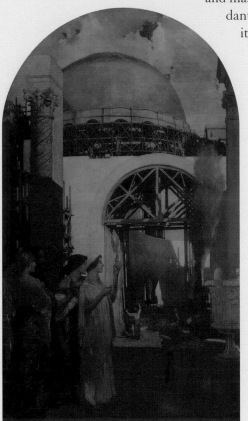

THE SUBDUED, HARMONIC COLORS, flat surfaces and abstract subject of Arthur Mathews's mural *The Arts* (1917) are characteristic of the California Decorative Style, perfected and dominated by Mathews and his wife, Lucia Kleinhans Mathews, between 1890 and 1915.

To some, the trio of muses giving silent approval to a construction project seemed to etherealize machinery and feminize the muscular, masculine spirit exemplified by the bronze workmen, struggling to master a recalcitrant machine, in Douglas Tilden's Donahue Monument. Yet others have argued that the Mathews mural does not distort the true meaning of "mechanics" any more than Tilden's idealized workmen do. The mural, they say, suits the Mechanics' Institute as surely as its old-fashioned, sometimes misunderstood name. A mechanic, as Andrew Hallidie pointed out, is a *creator*, not merely a person with a technical skill. For many years, the Institute used a bookplate based on a sketch by Mathews. The mechanics are at work, but the muses are absent.

Rudolph J. Taussig, who served the Institute ten years as president and twenty-two years as a trustee, donated the Mathews painting that was destroyed in the fire. Apparently he also paid Mathews $2100 to paint and frame the allegorical mural. Taussig, like the art he admired, exemplified the changing perspective and purposes of the Mechanics' Institute. He was a generalist, a cosmopolitan, an art lover, a devotee of the City Beautiful style of municipal grandeur. His family were liquor dealers, artists and businessmen. Taussig himself was as different from Andrew Hallidie, the practical engineer, as San Francisco's new mayor, the expansive, top-hatted executive "Sunny Jim" Rolph was from the goods-peddlers and money changers who ran the town during the gold rush.

When San Francisco received international approval for an exposition in 1915 to celebrate the completion of the Panama Canal, Taussig became a director and secretary of the Exposition Company. Joseph M. Cumming, who had been secretary of the Mechanics' Institute, was hired to the paid position of executive secretary. (The then-president Livingston Jenks boasted that "it was the Mechanics' Institute that taught San Francisco how to conduct fairs.")

Taussig's cultural leadership was recognized by the American Historical Association, which invited him to speak at its national meeting during the Exposition. In respect for the alleged theme of the fair, Taussig read a paper called "The Development of the Canal Idea." In truth, the Exposition was a celebration of the city's recovery after the earthquake and fire. Even the outbreak of war in Europe did not dim the lights.

THE PALACE OF FINE ARTS, by the Berkeley architect Bernard Maybeck, was the most beautiful and popular building of the Panama Pacific International Exposition (February 20–December 4, 1915). Built originally of light slats and tinted stucco, it has been patched, painted and twice reconstructed in permanent materials. At age ninety, it remains one of the most beloved and photographed structures in San Francisco.

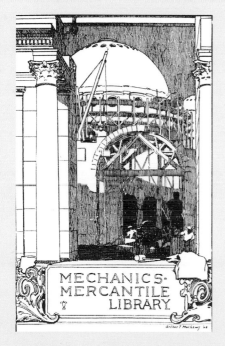

MATHEWS'S FIRST DOME was drawn in 1906 as a bookplate for the combined libraries of the Mechanics' Institute and the Mercantile Association. It shows workers constructing a classic palace with Corinthian columns like those designed by Bernard Maybeck for the colonnade of the Palace of Fine Arts in 1915. The Mechanics' used the plate until the merger contract expired in 1956.

A CLASSICAL LANDSCAPE WITH FIGURES outside a temple girded with scaffolds was Arthur Mathews's original concept for the vestibule of the Mechanics' Library. The mural, a gift to the Institute from Rudolph J. Taussig, was destroyed in the 1906 disaster and replaced eleven years later by *The Arts*, the allegorical wall painting in the current building.

An era scarred by war

YEARS OF INVENTION, INTERVENTION AND SPECULATION

1915   The first transcontinental telephone call takes place on January 25, from Alexander Graham Bell, the inventor of the telephone, in New York, to Thomas Watson, his onetime assistant, in San Francisco. During the call, Bell repeats his famous first words: "Mr. Watson, come here, I want you." Watson answers: "It would take me a week now."

1916   A bomb thrown at the Preparedness Day Parade on Market Street (July 22) kills ten and injures forty people. Radical labor leaders Thomas Mooney and Warren Billings are tried and imprisoned but years later are found to be innocent of the crime.

1917   The city's new main library (cost $1.153 million, capacity 500,000 to one million volumes) opens on February 15 … The United States enters World War I on April 16.

1918   The University of California constructs an office building at 130 Sutter Street, designed by Willis Polk and named to honor longtime Mechanics' Institute president and U.C. regent Andrew S. Hallidie.

1919   Maestro Gaetano Merola leads the formation of the San Francisco Opera Company.

1920   The Eighteenth Amendment takes effect in January, but San Francisco's attitude toward prohibition is described by one enforcement officer as "hilarious non-compliance" … In mid-summer (June 28–July 6) the Democratic National Convention meets at the Civic Auditorium, nominates Governor James M. Cox of Ohio for president and former New York State Senator Franklin Delano Roosevelt for vice president.

1921   Civilian pilots Jack Knight and Ernest M. Allison fly the first airmail from San Francisco to New York in 33 hours and 20 minutes.

1921   Dashiell Hammett gets a job as a detective at the Pinkerton Agency in the Flood Building on Market Street, where he begins gathering material for his celebrated stories of private investigator Sam Spade, meanwhile writing advertising copy for a jeweler at $100 a month.

THE HALLIDIE BUILDING (1918), an architectural gem and designated city landmark, is believed to be the world's first structure with a glass curtain wall.

SAN FRANCISCO MUNICIPAL AIRPORT was officially opened in May, 1927, although various types of aircraft had been landing and taking off on the same mushy, bayside pasture for several years. Known originally as Mills Field, the airport took its name from the banker Darius Ogden Mills, who once owned most of the Spanish rancho BuriBuri, now occupied by the airport as well as by South San Francisco, San Bruno, Millbrae and part of Burlingame. In that record-setting year, Charles Lindbergh made his famous solo flight across the Atlantic. His triumphal cross-country tour included a parade (in a car, not a plane) in San Francisco.

1922 Radio stations proliferate in the Bay Area, invading one another's channels with phonograph records transmitted from Telegraph Hill, office buildings and department stores.

1923 O'Shaughnessy Dam in the Hetch Hetchy Canyon of the Tuolumne River is completed after three decades of political controversy over the city's efforts to secure a water supply (and saleable electric power) from the Sierra … In August, President Warren G. Harding dies unexpectedly and mysteriously in his room at the Palace Hotel. General John J. "Black Jack" Pershing, on a visit to his former command post at the San Francisco Presidio, is called to accompany the casket to Washington, D.C.

1924 An experimental day-and-night airmail service between San Francisco and New York begins on a 2680-mile route (August) … The California Palace of the Legion of Honor, dedicated to the memory of Californians killed in World War I, opens on the anniversary of the Armistice ending the "War to End All Wars."

1926 Philo Farnsworth, a twenty-year-old college dropout, working in a small research laboratory at the foot of Telegraph Hill, develops the cathode ray tube that is the basis of television … The Mark Hopkins Hotel, in the style of a French château nineteen stories high, opens in December on the site of the forty-room mansion of Mark Hopkins, one of the "Big Four" railroad financiers.

1927 The San Francisco Airport (Mills Field) in San Mateo County is dedicated … Later in the year, Charles Lindbergh visits San Francisco on a triumphal tour celebrating his solo flight across the Atlantic.

1929 The crash of stock prices in October signals a precipitous downturn in the American economy, leading to the Great Depression of the 1930s.

LOCAL AND IMPORTED CHAMPIONS PLAY THE GAME

After the devastation of 1906, the Mechanics' Chess Room was back in action sooner than the library. Chess boards were set up in a corner of the temporary building before any books were on the shelves. Very few players admitted they had experienced a temporary loss of concentration.

An Army sergeant stationed at Fort Miley, on the Pacific headlands looking westward toward the San Andreas Fault, confessed in a letter to a chess magazine that the terror of the experience had driven chess completely out of his mind for an entire week, from April 18 to April 25.

"On the latter date," he wrote, "I received a postal with moves in a correspondence game, and, truthfully, the notations seemed Greek to me for a moment."

In their room in the new building on Post Street (which turned out to be on the third instead of the fourth floor), the chess players could again hold statewide tournaments, stage telegraph matches, ponder problems posed by senior players and entertain foreign champions. Their status as the leading club in western America was guaranteed by a quiet, comfortable, secluded place to play and a membership of skilled, contentious amateurs, eager to take on masters from around the world.

Reigning champions stopped at the Mechanics' to demonstrate their power by challenging (and

EARLY IN THE TWENTIETH CENTURY, when the telegraph line was the cheapest, fastest, most accessible means of communication up and down the Pacific Coast, San Francisco and Los Angeles held yearly chess matches on a dedicated line with a telegraph key at each end. In the tournament pictured (May 30, 1926), fifteen men pondered their moves in the Chess Room of the Mechanics' Institute while fifteen opponents faced them in Los Angeles. Each player wrote each move on a slip of paper, and a messenger at the far end of the room carried it to the telegrapher, who sat at the key with a line to Los Angeles dangling from the ceiling. The telegrapher transmitted each outgoing move to Los Angeles and skewered the slip of paper on a spindle numbered for the appropriate board. The response from Los Angeles was written down and passed to the player. After the play, the paper came back to join the pile on the spindle, forming a move-by-move record of the game. Pairs of clocks imposed time limits to avoid the agonizing delays and the sometimes-deliberate stalling of the first telegraph tournaments. The outcome of this encounter—the last of thirteen years of telegraph matches—was San Francisco, 8½ games to Los Angeles, 6½ games. (The half represents a draw.) In later years, the rivalry would continue in a series of face-to-face encounters in Atascadero and San Luis Obispo, mid-points on the newly surfaced automobile road along the route of the old Camino Real between northern and Southern California.

THE BRILLIANT, TWENTY-FIVE-YEAR-OLD Cuban prodigy José Raúl Capablanca (left), who learned chess at four by watching his father play (and correcting his moves), humbled all his opponents at the Mechanics' in the spring of 1916 by scoring forty-six wins and three draws in a series of lightning games. The honor of the San Francisco club was upheld, more or less, by the three players who scored draws: George Hallwegen, James O. Chilton and Adolph J. Fink, twenty-six (right), the Mechanics' renowned problem composer and a future champion of California. Five years later, in 1921, Capablanca became world champion by defeating the great Emanuel Lasker. For eight consecutive years (1916–23) Capablanca was undefeated. He finally lost his title in 1927 to the Russian master Alexander Alekhine. Chess historian Terry Crandall records that Capablanca, having won every game but one in a large demonstration of simultaneous chess in Moscow, scored only a draw against a twelve-year-old boy to whom Capablanca said: "One day you will be champion." The boy, Mikhail Botvinnik (later known to the chess world as "The Great Stone Face"), did become world champion in 1948, having defeated Capablanca on the way. A. J. Fink was beaten by another Mechanics' player, Elmer W. Gruer, in the first-ever California championship competition in 1921. A year later he won the title and held it for three years after. He gained an international reputation as a composer of hundreds of published chess problems, an expert in endgame studies and an adjudicator of adjourned games. Innumerable players counted on Fink to settle their disagreements. The standing advice was "Send it to Fink."

usually defeating) the best California could offer. Spectators crowded the Chess Room to watch multi-game matches that were reported like sporting events in the daily newspapers.

Frank J. Marshall, who ruled for thirty years as United States Chess Champion, visited the Mechanics' in 1913 and 1915. On his first visit, he played simultaneous games with thirty-one challengers, including nine-year-old Marie Silvius. Only one member of the club, Bernardo Smith, was able to defeat Marshall. Miss Silvius and four others secured draws. On his second cross-country tour, the champion lost eight games to members of the club and settled for four draws. Marshall's reputation and his prodigious memory survived the blow. He was the first grand master to play 100 simultaneous games, and later tackled 155 opponents at one time, scoring 126 wins and 21 draws in seven hours. A week later, it was said, he could replay 153 of the games from memory but feared he was losing his mind because he had forgotten two.

During San Francisco's exposition year, 1915, the Serbian grand master Boris Kostic stormed in and out several times, defeating everyone he met before resuming his tour of several dozen North American cities. In the words of the *American Chess Bulletin*: "His extraordinary brilliancies have captivated chess lovers wherever he went." When the Polish prodigy Sammy Reshevsky, eleven, made his first tour of the United States in 1921, the Mechanics' Arthur Stamer, who scored a draw, was the only San Franciscan to escape defeat.

The longtime world champion Emanuel Lasker revisited San Francisco in 1926, almost a quarter-century after his earlier triumphs; and Alexander Alekhine, one of the world's five original grandmasters, visited the club on two American tours, before and after he took the world title from Capablanca in 1927. The Russian champion recalled that, on his second tour in 1929, he had encountered the strongest opposition "in San Francisco, in a place called the Mechanics' Institute."

A YOUNG PLAYER'S
ADMIRING VIEW OF AN OLD CLUB

Guthrie "Mac" McClain was a twenty-one-year-old senior at the University of California and deep into the game of chess when he came over from Berkeley one evening in early May, 1929, to watch Alexander Alekhine, the world champion, take on forty-three challengers in simultaneous games at the Mechanics' Chess Club. McClain could not afford the $2 fee for a board of his own, so he stood and watched the strongest players in Northern California treat Alekhine to eight defeats and eight draws against only twenty-seven wins. Years later, McClain recalled that epic night (the "simul" lasted from 8:30 P.M. till 2:30 A.M.) and wondered whether it was the strength of the Bay Area players or the famous "hospitality" of the club that had downed the Russian grandmaster, a noted bon vivant.

McClain became a top player; an influential chess editor; the leading organizer and manager of chess tournaments in northern California; and a life member and trustee (1980–83) of the Mechanics' Institute. He always remembered the look of the place as it first struck him:

THE MECHANICS' CHESS ROOM as McClain saw it in the 1930s.

> *Everything about the chess rooms seemed exciting to me. There were forty inlaid oak chess tables and forty big sets of chessmen, handmade of lignum vitae. [This wood came from a shipyard owned by one of the trustees, where it was used on the launching ways.] There were also some strange instruments called chess clocks—the first ones I had ever seen....*
>
> *There was a wall board where [Adolph J.] Fink always had a problem set up for testing before publication, and there was a notebook kept by Valentine Huber, which was full of historic games and interesting positions from encounters in the big room....*
>
> *The Mechanics' Institute had a built-in advantage over other clubs in that it owned its own building and operated under an endowment which paid 75 percent of the cost of each member. The membership fee in 1929 was only $6 per year, and remained that for more than forty years. Open every day, it became a second club for members of other chess clubs for miles around. It was the site for state championship tournaments and interclub team matches, as well as its own slate of tournaments. However, [the Mechanics' club] had a not-so-silent majority who preferred offhand games and became irritated with the tournaments that brought strangers into the club and imposed silence.*

THE "STRANGE INSTRUMENTS CALLED CHESS CLOCKS" that puzzled young "Mac" McClain are like a pair of stopwatches combined with an alarm clock. Chess Director John Donaldson sits here with an old-fashioned clock, capturing his opponent's black pawn. As each player completes a move, he stops his own clock and starts his opponent's clock. A player who fails to make the required number of moves within an agreed time— say, forty moves in two hours—loses on time.

LOSING
MEMBERS TO
THE ETHER

IN 1924, early in the prosperous decade now called the Jazz Age, the Mechanics' Institute offered a prophetic course of lectures by Herbert E. Metcalf, a former Navy pilot who had gained a niche in the history of technology by broadcasting a speech of President Woodrow Wilson from an airplane equipped with an electronic loudspeaker. Metcalf was working for a small company called Magnavox, marketing arc radio transmitters and vacuum tubes, essential components of radio broadcasting. Metcalf's series of lectures was titled, simply, "Radio."

In that year there were about a dozen radio stations in the Bay Area—ephemeral, experimental, low-voltage transmitters on the roofs of department stores and downtown office buildings and high places like Telegraph Hill. They sent sound through the air that you could hear on your own radio, if you had one—bits of news, weather reports and music from phonograph records and hotel dance bands. The range of broadcasting was short and the sound was scratchy. The likelihood that radio would become the world's most important form of communication for the next quarter-century was not immediately obvious. That it might also take over people's time for reading did not raise alarm at the Mechanics' Institute. The Library had been increasing its value to its subscribers with new holdings in business, engineering and science to keep up with California's new industries—petroleum, hydroelectric power and automobile manufacture.

In the quiet way of elderly, substantially endowed institutions, the Mechanics' celebrated its seventy-fifth anniversary in 1930 by publishing a short history of itself and doing some minor remodeling—better lighting, more space for chess, bright new paint in the reading room (ivory to replace the gloomy dark green) and shelf space for the forty thousand additional volumes the library expected to buy in the next six or seven years.

Since the great disaster of 1906, the library had grown every year. The membership, which peaked at 5008 in 1924, had eased down by only a few hundred by 1930. The treasury was rich in cash, bonds and real estate totaling $774,300. The collections had grown from nothing in April, 1906, to more than 109,000 volumes—not vast, as modern libraries go, but carefully chosen and largely catalogued.

The trouble was, the whole nation was plunging into deep economic depression. Hundreds of thousands of Californians were out of work. Office space stood vacant, and even reductions in rent did not create tenants. In his report to the members early in 1932, the president of the Institute, Dr. Arthur W. Scott, admitted, "The outlook for the coming year at this time is not so cheerful."

The "not so cheerful" year 1932 was as bad as Dr. Scott had feared. His successor, the longtime trustee and board secretary Joseph Cumming, reported that membership had fallen by 333, and vacancies and reductions in rent had cut revenues "to a considerable extent." He was pleased to report, however, that none of the bonds in the treasury had defaulted.

Year after year, the membership declined, and the remaining members checked out fewer books. Fiction, which had been everyone's favorite cheap entertainment, fell abruptly from favor.

At the beginning of the 1940s, the library could boast more than 142,000 volumes. The dues remained only $6 a year. But the Institute had suffered a net loss of 1200 members—almost a fourth of its membership—and the circulation of fiction continued to fall. In 1942, the president, George U. Hind, acknowledged that the decline in circulation probably was "attributable to the fact that the time heretofore spent in reading has been much lessened by the use of the radio."

The trustees, presumably, were using the radio, too, to listen to President Franklin Roosevelt's "Fireside Chats" as well as locally produced favorites: "Blue Monday Jamboree" with Al Pearce and His Gang; live sportscasts from KFRC; and, most riveting of all, Carleton E. Morse's "One Man's Family," the story of the Barbour family of Sea Cliff, the longest-running of all domestic dramas, second in national popularity only to the daily "Breakfast Club."

A BITTER STRIKE, TWO BRIDGES AND A FINAL FAIR

1932 A new city-county charter, the first revision of local government since 1900, comes into effect and almost immediately is subjected to the first of hundreds of revisions that swell the text to more than 110,000 words…Franklin Delano Roosevelt is elected president.

1932 The newly completed War Memorial Opera House on Van Ness Avenue opens with a performance of Giacomo Puccini's *Tosca*, conducted by Gaetano Merola. The following year, the San Francisco Opera forms a ballet school that develops over the next seventy years into the San Francisco Ballet, one of the world's leading dance companies.

1933 Coit Tower, the nozzle-shaped monument bequeathed to the city by the firemen's friend Lillie Hitchcock Coit, opens atop Telegraph Hill. Down on Broadway at the base of the hill, the end of Prohibition allows a mild revival of the infamous Barbary Coast euphemistically called the "International Settlement."

1934 Alcatraz Island, a former Army base, becomes a federal prison for the country's most notorious criminals, including Chicago's gang leader Al Capone, George "Machine Gun" Kelly and the famous "Birdman," Robert Stroud.

JOSEPH P. DIMAGGIO, a nineteen-year-old fresh from the playgrounds of North Beach, hit in a record-breaking sixty-one successive games in his rookie year, 1933, with the San Francisco Seals. The Seals had opened their new stadium at 16th and Bryant Streets two years earlier, in April, 1931, and won the championship of the Pacific Coast League that year. Sold to the New York Yankees in 1935, DiMaggio compiled a .325 lifetime batting average during thirteen years in the major leagues—and, in the season of 1941, a 56-game hitting streak.

"CLIPPER" PASSENGER SERVICE on Pan American Airways Sikorsky S-42 between San Francisco and Honolulu began in 1936, the year the Bay Bridge opened to vehicles and commuter trains, and a year before the dedication of the Golden Gate Bridge.

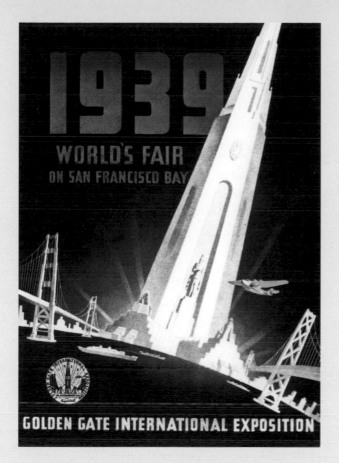

1939 WORLD'S FAIR ON SAN FRANCISCO BAY

GOLDEN GATE INTERNATIONAL EXPOSITION

THE GOLDEN GATE INTERNATIONAL EXPOSITION on Treasure Island (February 18–October 28, 1939) showed masterpieces of European and American art, model mines, futurist automobiles, flower gardens and an immense, outdoor "Cavalcade of the Golden West"—but what most people talked about was "Sally Rand's Nude Ranch." During the fair, Germany's invasion of Poland precipitated World War II in Europe. The fair reopened in 1940 with such added attractions as Billy Rose's Aquacade, Folies Bergère, "Cavalcade of America," and brilliant night lighting, and recouped some of the money lost in 1939. The last night (September 29) moved the newspaper columnist Herb Caen to write: "When the magnificent lights blacked out forever…you knew, suddenly, that an era had ended for a generation that would never be young again."

1934 A strike by longshoremen on the San Francisco waterfront escalates into a regional general strike and a bloody confrontation on July 5 between picketing workers and hired strike breakers in which two strikers are killed.

1934 Driven by a self-imposed challenge to write one story every day, William Saroyan turns out *The Daring Young Man on the Flying Trapeze*, the collection that led to his international fame.

1936 In the movie *San Francisco* a singer named Mary Blake (Jeanette MacDonald) works in the Barbary Coast gambling den of Blackie Norton (Clark Gable) against the advice of Father Tim Mullin (Spencer Tracy). The film displays

Hollywood's special effects in a scary interpretation of the 1906 quake which gives the impression that San Francisco is a dangerous place to live in, but full of joy if you survive.

1937 The Golden Gate Bridge opens to traffic.

1938 Treasure Island, site of an international exposition, is under construction by the US Army Corps of Engineers in the shallows north of Yerba Buena Island in San Francisco Bay.

1939 Attorney General Frank Murphy, a mainstay of Franklin D. Roosevelt's New Deal administration and later a justice of the Supreme Court, calls for closing the federal penitentiary on Alcatraz. The prison is finally closed in 1963.

The Ritz Old Poodle Dog, a contemporary version of one of San Francisco's oldest French restaurants, leased street-front space from the Mechanics' Institute in 1934 and, for the next forty-six years, became a landmark associated with the Library. According to local legend, its eponymous ancestor was named *Poulet d'Or* but was corrupted to *Poodle Dog* by thick-tongued Americans. Operated on increasingly disputatious terms by various members of the Calixte-LaLanne family, the restaurant closed in 1980 after the death of Mrs. LaLanne. Roberta M. Thomson, a life member of the Institute, recalled a "fragrant memory" of the Ritz Old Poodle Dog that ascended into the second-floor reading room. "Its pungent French cuisine fumes, wafting into the mezzanine's small loft [where I was researching family history], usually became a bit much, causing me to lose interest in food."

KEEPERS OF TRADITION IN CHANGING TIMES

WEAKENED BY LOSS of members, rents and investment income during the the Depression and the early years of World War II, the Institute survived on its accumulated wealth in real estate and bonds—and on the hard work of a dismally underpaid staff. An example of matchless institutional loyalty was that of Joseph Cumming, who, as secretary to the board during the 1906 disaster, had saved the archives from devastation and then rounded up the trustees and helped recreate the library in temporary quarters among the ruins. After fourteen years in a paid position, Cumming served three decades as a member of the unpaid board of trustees.

MARY CARMODY,
chief librarian, 1935–48.

Mary Carmody was the first woman to serve as chief librarian for the Institute, and she stepped into one of its most difficult periods—from 1935 until 1948, the years of the Great Depression, World War II and its unsettled aftermath—a time of tight budgets, depleted staffs and dwindling membership. Mrs. Carmody, who had joined the staff in 1918 as a research librarian, maintained the quality of personal service that endeared the Mechanics' Library to its members. She became a friend to innumerable writers who came to the reading room to browse or work or get out of the cold.

After she retired in 1948 to devote herself to gardening, reading and travel, she gave an interview in which she recalled: "Just about every writer of any distinction who ever wrote in the city was a member. It was an illustrious roster, and wonderful to know them, and watch them work."

She remembered Jack London, a favorite of the staff, although "inclined to be a bit careless about returning books," and John Cowper Powys and Charles Caldwell Dobie and Stewart Edward White, prolific novelists in the thirties, when everyone read novels and writers fancied triple names.

She was pestered one day by a demanding young man who insisted on seeing some New York newspapers that were in storage.

"But he wasn't a member, and we couldn't go running down to the basement for him," Mrs. Carmody said. It was only later that someone told her the pesky young man was William Saroyan.

"None of us recognized him. He was too neatly dressed."

John Stump, who had been a staff librarian through the thirties and into the war years, when he took leave to

LIBRARIAN JOHN STUMP
with minutes saved
from the 1906 fire.

join the Army, succeeded Mary Carmody as head librarian in 1949. A man of many talents—an athlete, musician, painter, writer and student of history—Stump liked talking with the members, recommending books, tracking down information, suggesting leads. He became a meticulous archivist, gathering and preserving the rare and fragile records that formed the basis for a commemorative pamphlet on the hundredth anniversary of the Institute.

SECRETARY JOSEPH CUMMING at his desk in 1911.

CRIES OF WAR AND PEACE

1940 Census figures for the decade 1930–40 show no growth in San Francisco (634,349 vs. 634,536) and a small percentage increase in Oakland, which had more than doubled in population after the earthquake and fire of 1906.

1941 Japanese bombers attack the U.S. Naval Base at Pearl Harbor and other American military installations in the Pacific, dragging a shocked and unready nation into the global war.

1942 Japanese and Japanese American residents of coastal areas are evacuated to inland relocation camps.

1943 President Franklin D. Roosevelt urges—and achieves—repeal of the Chinese Exclusion Act, in force in various forms since 1882.

1944 Kaiser Shipyards in Richmond assembles and launches the Liberty ship USS *Robert E. Peary* in five days in a competition with other American shipyards. During the 1365 days in World War II, the thirty shipyards in the Bay Area produce 1400 vessels.

1945 A formative conference of the United Nations, called together in anticipation of the end of World War II, convenes at the Civic Center from April through June.

1946 Two guards and three prisoners are killed in a revolt at Alcatraz prison.

1946 The San Francisco 49ers, the first extension of the fledgling All-America Football Conference to the West Coast, are founded by Tony Morabito, a local businessman.

1948 The first telecast in San Francisco on May 25 is followed by a sudden proliferation of broadcast television on three commercial channels—KPIX (December 24, 1948), KGO (May 25, 1949) and KRON (November, 1949). Two other UHF stations in the San Francisco–Oakland area open later: KQED, one of the nation's first public stations, in 1954 and KTVU in 1958.

CAUSE FOR CELEBRATION: When news of the Japanese surrender reached the city on August 15, 1945, a cheering crowd poured into the streets and congealed into an all-night party that stretched from the Ferry Building to the foot of Twin Peaks. Perched on a ladder at Mason and Market Streets, a photographer pointed his camera eastward and captured a few thousand people at a moment of reckless joy—never to be equaled, repeated or forgotten.

THE MECHANICS' CHESS CLUB
CHECKMATES THE BOARD

The trustees denied it was true, but the members of the Mechanics' Chess Club, ever protective of their fourth-floor domain, sensed a threat to their turf. The war was over, and the Institute was sprucing up its neglected building, buying books and reaching out to new members. Someone complained that the chess players were shabbily dressed. They lacked couth. The Chess Room must go!

The alarm reached Robert O'Brien, who wrote a daily column of historic anecdotes in the *San Francisco Chronicle*. O'Brien came to the defense with an exaggerated but effective plea for the "small and intent, but harmless" chess players whose historic, world-famous game room might be closed forever by a bunch of money-minded trustees who wanted rental income from the space.

BLACK HAS WHITE in checkmate in this W.A. Cameron drawing that accompanied Robert O'Brien's 1948 column in defense of the "unkempt" habitués of the Mechanics' Chess Club.

"The stated reason," O'Brien wrote in his popular "Riptides" column (April 5, 1948), "is that some of the devotees of the game of kings, riding up to their rendezvous...leave something to be desired in the way of sartorial distinction. In brief, backers of the plan say, some of them look, and are, unkempt."

O'Brien traced the Chess Room back to the founding of the Institute "for the working-man, and to foster a feeling of social friendship among the members." He reported that old-timers thought it "strange" that one of the most democratic gathering places in the city should be threatened because some of its habitués were messy dressers, and he invoked the names of the great visitors—Frank J. Marshall, Harry Pillsbury, Alexander Alekhine, José R. Capablanca —and of the current star, Charles Bagby, as proof of the value of the club to humanity. The *Chronicle*'s powerful items-columnist Herb Caen heated up the controversy with a stinging quip: "The Mechanics is trying to pull its chess-nuts out of the foyer."

The trustees, if they had such an evil intention, publicly disclaimed it and beat a fast retreat. The idea was buried at the next membership meeting. In his report on the year's accomplishments, Board President Elgin Stoddard pointed out that the Chess Room had received a "complete refurbishing [and now] is a room of which our members may well be proud." He said nothing about a dress code. Bagby, a well-dressed attorney and later state champion, was elected to the board of trustees for the eighth time.

A later board, in response to a petition from the Chess Club, added to the constitution of the Institute the words "There shall be a Chess Room." As if to validate this pledge over the next fifty-seven years, a number of active chess players—including Bagby, Ralph Hultgren, Neil Falconer, Guthrie McClain, Bob Burger, Mark Pinto and Vince McCambridge— have been elected trustees. Several have served as president of the Institute.

DUKES OF THE ROYAL GAME

CHARLES BAGBY (RIGHT) AND VLADIMIR "WALTER" PAFNUTIEFF, longtime friends and competitors, were powers in the Chess Room for four decades. Russian-born Pafnutieff, who immigrated to California via China in 1930, became the Mechanics' representative in many team competitions. Energetic and talented, he sang in opera (bass-baritone), coached tennis (Rosie Casals, among others) and wrote a successfully published textbook on chess. Bagby, a trial lawyer, was chess champion of California in 1958, but he was, perhaps, more renowned for his encyclopedic knowledge of subjects small and large (the major landmarks of Shawnee and Tecumseh, Oklahoma, for example, or last year's net tonnage through San Francisco harbor) and for his nonstop monologues. Except for J. J. Dolan (of San Francisco Endgame fame), who was a trustee from 1910 to 1913, Bagby was the first—and for many years the only—chess player to be elected to the Mechanics' board of trustees. From 1941 until his death in 1975, a record thirty-five years, Bagby was the voice and ears of the Chess Club on the board. He was second vice president for twelve years, although he was never accorded the presidency, which would have made him a regent of the University of California. Among Bagby's most celebrated encounters were his ten-game challenge match with the unflappable and reputedly unconquerable Adolph J. Fink in 1939, which ended in a 5–5 draw, and a bitterly contested tournament for the Mechanics' championship, in which Bagby finished second to Earl Pruner. More important, perhaps, in the tight world of chess: Bagby was among the immortal eight who beat the great Alexander Alekhine during his humbling simul-match at the Mechanics' in 1929. Alekhine said Bagby's game was the best of the night.

THE DUTCH MASTER MACHGIELIS "MAX" EUWE (whose name, pronounced *uhr-vuh*, is a shibboleth, like the town Scheveningen, for the correct pronunciation of Dutch names) was unique among chess players for his stature (6'4"), his breadth of interest (he held a doctorate in mathematics and went in for flying, swimming and boxing) and his lifelong amateur status. In his year of glory, 1935, Euwe took the official world championship from the formidable Alexander Alekhine, who won it back in 1937. Bobby Fischer said of Euwe after playing two games to a tie score: "That man is too normal. There must be something wrong with him."

In a four-hour show at the Mechanics' Chess Club in January, 1949, Euwe won sixteen of his twenty-two simultaneous games, lost three (to Paul Wolf, seventeen-year-old Herbert Dashel of San Francisco and Robert T. Konkel of Richmond) and drew three (with Charles Bagby and Neil E. Falconer of the Mechanics' and Charles Svalberg of the Russian Chess Club).

BEATS AND BUILDINGS

1951 In September, Prime Minister Yoshida Shigeru of Japan, in a ceremony at San Francisco's War Memorial Opera House, signs the United States–Japan Security Treaty, officially ending the war in the Pacific.

1951 Restaurateur Enrico Banducci opens his hungry i (for "hungry id") nightclub, the launching place of comedians Mort Sahl, Lenny Bruce, Woody Allen and Bill Cosby, and musicians Barbra Streisand and The Limeliters.

1954 San Francisco International Airport opens.

1956 The Republican National Convention convenes at the Cow Palace (August 20–28) and nominates incumbent President Dwight D. Eisenhower and, for vice president, Senator Richard M. Nixon of California.

1957 With voter approval, the California legislature establishes the five-county Bay Area Rapid Transit District (BART) to design and build a transbay and intracity passenger travel system.

1957 The most severe earthquake since 1906 strikes the Bay Area on March 22, registering 5.53 on the Richter scale. No deaths or serious injuries result, and structural damage is largely confined to the southwest edge of the city.

1958 The New York Giants move their National League baseball franchise to San Francisco, and the Brooklyn Dodgers move simultaneously to Los Angeles, bringing major-league competition for the first time to the Pacific Coast.

1959 Avery Brundage, twenty-year president of the International Olympic Committee, donates a large share of his magnificent collection of Chinese, Japanese, South Asian and Himalayan objects to the seedling Asian Art Museum.

1960 Candlestick Park, a 70,000-seat multipurpose stadium, opens as a home for the National League San Francisco Giants. It later becomes the home park for the NFL 49ers.

LAWRENCE FERLINGHETTI

GARY SNYDER

JACK KEROUAC

ALLEN GINSBERG

POETS AND NOVELISTS OF "THE BEAT GENERATION" (Jack Kerouac, Gary Snyder, Allen Ginsberg, Gregory Corso) found a spiritual base in the early 1950s at Lawrence Ferlinghetti's City Lights Book Store on Columbus Avenue and in his paperback Pocket Poets series. Ferlinghetti's most memorable (and controversial) publication was Allen Ginsberg's *Howl* (1956), a torrent of unrhymed existential despair. Temporarily suppressed by zealous police on grounds of obscenity, *Howl* was ultimately cleared in a precedent-setting court decision. Ginsberg gave the first public reading of the poem at the Six Gallery, an art space in a former auto repair shop at Union and Fillmore Streets. Onstage were the young poets Snyder, Michael McClure and Philip Whalen; the senior poet, Kenneth Rexroth, who had organized the reading; and Kerouac, whose 1957 novel *On the Road* was destined to provide a collective name—"the Beats"—for the group and its hangers-on. While Ginsberg read, Kerouac punctuated each stanza by pounding a jug of wine at the edge of the stage.

THE CROWN ZELLERBACH BUILDING, a glistening twenty-story cube of blue-green glass in a triangular plaza at Bush, Sansome and Market Streets, was completed in 1959, the first office tower after World War II.

THE SAN FRANCISCO CHRONICLE'S "CRUSADE" against naked animals was launched, tongue in cheek, by the mischievous editor Scott Newhall in the summer doldrums of 1962. A few readers, not recognizing a circulation-building stunt, were shocked; curiosity drew others to the growing paper.

1960 Police use clubs and fire hoses at San Francisco's City Hall to turn away demonstrators trying to crowd a hearing by the House Committee on Un-American Activities.

1962 The San Francisco Giants win their first National League baseball pennant.

1962 Groundbreaking for the Golden Gateway redevelopment project takes place on the site of the historic produce district.

1963 The federal penitentiary on Alcatraz Island is closed.

1963 Businessman Donald G. Fisher opens a specialty shop in a derelict street-front space on Ocean Avenue, near San Francisco City College. Selling only pop music records and Levi jeans, the shop is named "The Gap."

1963 The Republicans return to the Cow Palace for their national convention (July 13–16) and nominate Senator Barry M. Goldwater of Arizona for president and Representative William E. Miller of New York for vice president.

1963 A Dragon Gate is erected at Grant Avenue and Bush Street, on the southern edge of historic Chinatown.

1965 In August, the Beatles give the last concert of their last world tour at Candlestick Park.

SCENES FROM AN OASIS

We will do our best to continue furnishing a friendly, personal kind of library service to the community; to provide a quiet oasis, a place of refuge in the center of the noisy, crowded city, where one can escape for a time from the world of work and business, and find spiritual peace, refreshment and renewal in the world of books.

—Theodore R. Meyer, president of the Mechanics' Institute, in an address during National Library Week, 1964

IN THE EUPHORIC, easy-money Eisenhower years, it was easy to believe that the established institutions of literate society—the schools, the press, the libraries—would always retain their traditional audience and their historic respect, despite the profound social and economic changes of the war years, the restless mobility of a population of automobile drivers, and the absorbing, mesmerizing competition of television.

The Mechanics'-Mercantile Library in its centennial year, 1955, possessed approximately 155,000 books and countless thousands of pamphlets, monographs, documents and United States Government publications—all acquired, like its handsome headquarters building, after the devastation of 1906. There were about five thousand members, many living outside San Francisco. The library and the building were supervised by a seasoned, accommodating, highly professional staff. The Chess Club had its first full-time director, the honored and respected champion Arthur Stamer, who organized tournaments and exhibitions that filled the room with skillful players and excited spectators. At $6 a year, membership in the Mechanics' was not only a bargain but, as the columnist Herb Caen once observed, "The city's best-kept secret."

The leadership in those days was willing to maintain the secrecy, although they frequently announced that anyone could join—it was practically free. The fourteen trustees were all successful, conservative professionals and business leaders, drawn from the educated class of a comfortable, slow-moving, self-satisfied city, but they were glad to share the blessings of the club. They took pride in their measured judgment and their forward-looking management of

THE NAME ON THE DOOR and on the bookplates endured for fifty years after the two libraries merged, although almost no trace remained of the founding associations except their combined membership. Everyone spoke of it simply as "The Mechanics'" and thought of it as a sort of club. Theodore R. Meyer, a trustee for more than twenty years, declared: "Mechanics' Institute is a tradition. Families have belonged to it for generations. For some it is almost a home, or a way of life. Many would feel a great void in their lives if it did not exist."

THE VIEW SOUTHEAST FROM RUSSIAN HILL in 1944 (*left*) and 1974 (*right*) shows the effects of thirty years of upward growth. Still the same: the twin towers of the Church of Nuestra Señora de Guadalupe, on Broadway at Mason Street.

A NEW SKYLINE, A CHANGING CITY

1965 The *San Francisco Examiner* devours its triple-headed sister, the *News-Call-Bulletin*, moves to afternoon publication and starts putting out a joint Sunday edition with its old rival, the *Chronicle*. This mess is called the *Chron-Ex*.

1966 The *Bay Guardian* begins weekly publication in a newspaper world that is not destined to become braver or newer because of the competition.

1967 The first-ever Human Be-In, an epochal "Gathering of the Tribes" defining and displaying the characteristics of the counterculture, brings ten thousand hippies and hippy imitators to the Polo Field in Golden Gate Park.

1967 In April, antiwar demonstrators march from Second and Market Streets to Kezar Stadium to protest American involvement in Vietnam.

1967 The American Conservatory Theater (ACT), founded in Pittsburgh, Pennsylvania, by William Ball, moves to San Francisco.

NEW TOWERS: The Transamerica Pyramid (*right*), San Francisco's tallest building at 855 feet (1972), looks shorter than the 52-story Bank of America (1969) because it's three blocks farther away.

1969 Native Americans and sympathizers, led by self-appointed leader Richard Oakes, seize and occupy the vacant federal prison on Alcatraz Island, claimed by Sioux leaders as "unoccupied government land."

1969 George Lucas, twenty-five, a recent graduate of film school at the University of Southern California, directs his first feature film, *THX 1138*, with handheld cameras, natural light and a sparse budget.

1970 St. Mary's Roman Catholic Cathedral, at Geary Boulevard and Gough Street, is consecrated.

1971 U.S. marshals retake Alcatraz Island from the Native American occupation. Two years later the National Park Service begins a guided tour service to the island by boat from San Francisco.

1972 The federal government establishes the 72,000-acre Golden Gate National Recreation Area, a coastal preserve reaching 28 miles from the southwest edge of San Francisco to Point Reyes in northern Marin County.

THE NOBLE REGENCY MEETS AN IGNOBLE END

FOR OVER A HUNDRED YEARS, every president of the Mechanics' Institute during his term of office had also been an ex officio regent of the University of California. Few Californians knew or cared about the strange role of a small San Francisco library in the governance of the huge and growing state university. Those who did know generally considered the relationship a harmless academic anachronism, like graduation robes or diplomas written in Latin.

Over the years, twenty-five presidents of the Mechanics' had been U.C. regents. Many, including Andrew S. Hallidie, had distinguished business or professional careers and would easily have gained political appointment to the board of regents without their connection to the Institute. The two most recent—Theodore R. Meyer and Joseph A. Moore—both received gubernatorial appointments after their terms expired.

The Mechanics' traditional place in the regency suddenly became a touchy political issue in the early 1960s, when the demands of the student-led Free Speech Movement and other protest campaigns began to confound the administration of the Berkeley campus. The regents, as policy-makers for a multicampus university, were alarmed by the power of the nonviolent protesters to influence—even to close down—the system. Their response was to assert their authority and punish any administrator who appeared to yield to coercion. When Ronald Reagan took office as governor in January, 1966, having campaigned on a promise to end the turmoil in Berkeley, he appointed a slate of new regents committed to impose discipline on the university. The first act of the new board, chaired by Mechanics' representative Theodore Meyer, was to dismiss the president of the university, Clark Kerr.

By their intervention in Berkeley's problems, the regents became a stationary target of the protest movement. The Marxist journalist Bettina Aptheker, a close and sympathetic follower of the protest movement, wrote in *The Nation* (September 7, 1970): "Many of the worst crises and confrontations on the University of California campuses have been either provoked directly by the regents or aggravated by a punitive disciplinary policy. More important, very large numbers of students have been driven into a frustrated fury by the unresponsiveness of the regents, and of higher authorities, in general, to their demands, concerns and aspirations."

It occurred to some observers that a quick and easy way to share in the power of the regents would be to take over the Mechanics' Institute. Most of the trustees were outraged that anyone should attempt to drag Berkeley's ferocious ideological struggle into the orderly internal politics of the Institute.

Joseph Moore, who had been a trustee since 1951 and was president of the Mechanics' board from 1969 to 1974, recalled in an oral history some years later that the Mechanics' trustees had "never, never, never" tried to influence the actions of their representative on the board of regents.

"That's why I thought it was wrong for people like the students, or anybody else, to try and take over the Mechanics' Institute with no interest at all in the Mechanics' Institute. You should not become a trustee of the Mechanics' Institute…because you are interested to achieve some other result as a regent of the University of California."

Moore recalled with evident satisfaction the failure of a student group to seize command of the Institute. The *Daily Californian* newspaper, he said, had printed a facsimile of the Institute's application form and asked readers to send in a check for $7, which would be held until the campaign had collected 2700 applications. That would be enough, they calculated, to gain a majority in the next election of trustees. The response, according to Moore, was only seventeen paid applications, all but two of which were returned by the *Daily Cal* to the students a year later.

"Of those two, one girl later said she didn't really want to join. She got her money back. The net result of this immense amount of effort was one new member for the Mechanics' Institute."

The board also fought off an intramural campaign to seat Robert Gordon Sproul, Jr., as president. As the son of U.C.'s highly respected president for twenty-eight years (1930–58), Sproul added resonance to the Mechanics' election process. (The administration building and central plaza on the Berkeley campus, scene of most of the political demonstrations, were named for his father.) The challengers put together a slate to represent various interests—and, in a sense, to obscure their purpose—and Moore said he was not sure what they were after.

One faction wanted changes in management of the investments. Another wanted a different book selection, and others wanted more emphasis on chess.

"It's difficult for the board of trustees to run any organization so that somebody doesn't have some complaint about something," Moore said.

The Mechanics' board survived the insurrection as it had earlier rebellions, and the campaign to reform the board of regents moved to other political venues. Up and down the state, legislators were drafting amendments to Article IX, Section 9 of the state constitution, hoping to satisfy everyone, right and left, who thought there was something wrong with the way the regents got to be regents. All of the proposals suggested getting rid of those seats reserved for the president of the Mechanics' Institute of San Francisco and for the president of the State Board of Agriculture.

Proposition Four, a constitutional amendment revising the makeup of the regents, reached the voters in November, 1974. Under its detailed provisions, the governor would have two more appointments, but their terms would be reduced from sixteen years to twelve years. The governor would be required to consult an advisory committee in making the appointments, and the appointees would be required to reflect the economic, cultural and social diversity of the state, "including ethnic minorities and women." The regents themselves would be authorized to make one-year appointments of an enrolled student and an active faculty member. The vice president of the alumni association would become an ex officio regent. And the ex officio memberships of the president of the State Board of Agriculture and the president of the Mechanics' Institute of San Francisco would disappear.

A chief proponent of the measure was Charles J. Hitch, who had succeeded Clark Kerr as president of the university. The Mechanics' Institute did not file a ballot argument against the amendment. One state senator, John Stull, a Republican from San Diego,

urged the voters to reject the measure. He argued that it was "truly unwise" to remove the spokesman for agriculture, "because agriculture is California's number one industry (not counting government)." He did not mention the desirability of having a regent to speak for the mechanic arts.

The amendment passed by a convincing margin, 55.3 percent to 44.7 percent.

To most of the members and trustees of the Institute, the result was neither surprising nor unwelcome. It was obvious that the historic link between the Mechanics' and the university had been broken long ago by the growth and change in California, its economy and its educational system. The campaign to control the Institute in order to gain a seat on the regents had been embarrassing, disruptive and grotesque. Elder statesmen like Joseph Moore, who remained a member of the board of regents for sixteen additional years, did not like to think that the Mechanics' had been corrupted by outside political influence. Asked in his oral history about the motives of the dissidents, Moore said: "I cannot remember what, in that particular case where Mr. Sproul was a candidate, was their main item of concern...I cannot and I will not speculate as to anyone's motives."

At the annual membership meeting a month after the election, David J. McDaniel, the last president of the Institute to serve as a regent of the university (for six months), expressed no regret. The decision of the voters "in no way would affect the operations of the Institute," McDaniel said.

In truth, it cooled things down. Freed from the responsibility, the criticism and the pangs of guilt that went with their historic privilege, the trustees turned to other matters. None of them could hope now to be a regent of the university unless a future governor should be impressed with his extraordinary talents or his economic, social or cultural diversity. (Reagan had appointed both Meyer and Moore to further terms, although they were white, male, prosperous and middle-aged.) In any case, the trustees of the Institute had other concerns: How to make up the revenues lost in the collapse of the program of affinity flights? How to deal with an overgrown membership, puffed up by the offer of bargain airline fares? How to manage a portfolio of stock investments battered by recession? How to collect the rent from the Ritz Old Poodle Dog?

The awful seventies

A BAD DECADE WITH A TRAGIC END

I s this the nadir of our history as an American city, this decade of random violence, personal loss and despondency so paralyzing that it cripples our power to defend ourselves from the ravages of radical change? Our most venerable institutions of education, government and culture seem to be crumbling around us. The downtown financial district proliferates with dense new office towers while traffic congeals in the streets. Beloved landmarks disappear, and dependable old businesses fail or move away. We are stunned by the disaster of that strange, utopian church known as the People's Temple, whose leader Jim Jones preached brotherhood and salvation, and then herded his dazzled flock into a tropical wilderness and ordered them to deal themselves an agonizing death. Then, a few days later, our handsome young mayor is slain, and with him the small, intensely ambitious shopkeeper from Castro Street whose political success raised the expectations and self-esteem of that isolated minority who ironically called themselves "gay." What has happened to us? Where are we going?

—A letter from San Francisco, 1978

1973 The last American troops leave South Vietnam. The war has cost 58,000 American dead, 150,000 seriously wounded and 1000 missing in action. The Vietnamese toll is far higher.

1974 Richard M. Nixon resigns the presidency on August 9 … The San Francisco Giants close their season with a 9–5 loss to San Diego. There are more than 56,000 empty seats at Candlestick Park.

1974 Michael Tilson Thomas, twenty-nine, debuts with the San Francisco Symphony, conducting Gustav Mahler's *Ninth Symphony*. Thomas (known as "MTT") returns frequently to San Francisco before becoming the musical director of the symphony in 1995.

BAY TUBE OPENING—1974
FIRST RIDER TICKET

BART (BAY AREA RAPID TRANSIT)
TRAINS began their regular trans-bay service on September 16, 1974. The system, ultimately intended to link nine counties, now connects three.

1975 Joseph Alioto, a sleek, articulate, highly successful trial litigator, completes his second term as mayor of San Francisco. Haunted throughout his eight years in office by a libelous magazine article that incorrectly links him to the Sicilian mafia, Alioto finally wins vindication—and a $350,000 judgment —eleven years later, after four trials. "It should help stop the continuing slanders against Americans of Italian descent," he says after the verdict … North Vietnamese troops enter Saigon on August 30. Fifteen years of war in Vietnam finally end.

1975 Charles Schwab, in rented quarters on Montgomery Street, launches the first discount brokerage business with $100,000 of money borrowed from an uncle.

1975 Sara Jane Moore, a radical activist and would-be assassin, tries to fire a .38-caliber revolver at President Gerald Ford as he walks toward a speaking engagement at the St. Francis Hotel on September 22. Her hand is deflected by an ex-Marine named Oliver Sipple, who gains unwanted celebrity from the incident. Moore pleads guilty and is sent to prison for life.

1976 Patricia Campbell Hearst, twenty-one, is convicted of bank robbery after a two-month trial in San Francisco, where her grandfather, William Randolph Hearst, made the first few of his several million dollars as a newspaper publisher. Miss Hearst, who was kidnapped and held for two years by a band of ultra-radicals who styled themselves

VASSILY SMYSLOV, a former world champion (1958–60), took on thirty challengers on the evening of March 20, 1976, in one of the longest, best-attended simultaneous matches ever played in the Mechanics' Chess Club. The Russian-born master won eighteen games, gave nine draws and yielded three losses to teenaged players—Victor Baja, sixteen, of San Francisco; Randy Fong, seventeen, of Hayward; and Jay Whitehead, fourteen, of San Francisco. The most prolonged and difficult game pitted Smyslov against Neil Falconer, a longtime trustee of the Institute and leading member of the Chess Club. Late at night, Smyslov wore Falconer down in an ending.

BYE BYE BABY was Giants announcer Russ Hodges's trademark expression for a home run, in both New York and San Francisco. In this case, it was shortstop Tim Foli (wearing glasses) who lit up the scoreboard during a weak season (1977). He was congratulated by second baseman Rob Andrews and an admiring bat boy. The Giants continued to use Hodges's favorite exclamation in a lighted sign after the announcer's sudden death in 1971.

"The Symbionese Liberation Army," maintains that she had been coerced into helping in the robbery. Her jail sentence is later commuted by President Jimmy Carter and she is granted a full pardon by President Bill Clinton.

1977 The Oakland Raiders football team, coached by John Madden and quarterbacked by Ken Stabler, wins its first Super Bowl championship. Madden retires as head coach in 1979, and team owner Al Davis begins a three-year battle with the NFL to move the Raiders to Los Angeles.

1978 The Jonestown, Guyana, mass suicides and murders of adherents and observers of Jim Jones's People's Temple on November 18 stun and horrify the city. Less than ten days later, Mayor George Moscone and Supervisor Harvey Milk are shot and killed by Dan White, a onetime policeman and former supervisor. The two events are not related, but their cumulative impact leaves permanent wounds in the resilient fabric of the city.

1979 Dan White, convicted of murdering Mayor George Moscone and Supervisor Harvey Milk while in a state of "diminished capacity," is sentenced to seven years and eight months in prison. Released on parole in January, 1984, he resides for a year in Los Angeles before returning to San Francisco to live with his wife and family. In October, 1985, he hangs himself in the garage of his home.

1979 Willie Mays, the San Francisco Giants' great center fielder and league-leading hitter in the 1960s, is elected to the National Baseball Hall of Fame.

Freed (more or less) of the nervous apprehension that they might be pushed out by an unloving board of trustees, the Mechanics' chess players consolidated their position as the leading club in the West by establishing a year-round succession of tournaments and demonstrations and a program of classes and analytical conferences for learners.

The respected champion Arthur Stamer (for whom one of the major yearly tournaments is named) became the club's first official director in 1951. He was followed as director by Kurt Bendit, Howard Donnelly, William Addison, Alan Bourke, Ray Conway, Max Wilkerson, Jim Eade and John Donaldson.

In 1981 the Chess Room hosted a Northern California Chess Championship over three successive weekends. The tournament was the sixth in a series of Charles L. Bagby Memorial matches sponsored by the Mechanics' Institute, and chess historians rated it one of the strongest state championships (in terms of players and play) in American history. International Master John Grefe of Berkeley, who had won the United States Invitational Championship at age twenty-six in 1973, was a clear winner. Grefe remained a formidable player year after year, winning state championships in 1980, 1981, 1982 and 1995.

The first of several Pan Pacific Grandmaster tournaments convened at the Mechanics' in 1987. Between 1995 and 2003, there were six Grandmaster Invitational events and numerous tournaments offering strong young players the opportunity to develop their skills in competition with international masters. In the same period, the Chess Club attained a measure of long-term financial stability through a major bequest from the estate of Mrs. Charles Linklater. The Linklater gift created a permanent endowment, which has grown in value through additional gifts.

An occasional visitor to the Chess Room for half a century was the writer and tournament promoter George Koltanowski, whose column in the *San Francisco Chronicle* ran for fifty-two years. Koltanowski had made his reputation—and attained the rank of grandmaster—on the strength of his extraordinary memory, rather than his tournament skill. His world record of playing thirty-four simultaneous games while blindfolded, though unofficially challenged, has stood since 1937. Although he seldom won all his blindfold matches, Koltanowski usually could recall every move in every game.

WILLIAM ADDISON, director of the Mechanics' Chess Room (1965–69), and later a grandmaster, ponders a move (left) while younger players watch in respectful silence. When he pounces (right), that's when you have to ask yourself, What's he up to?

A GIFT FROM THIN AIR

AT THE PEAK OF THE MARKET for travel by affinity groups in the early 1970s, the Mechanics' Institute was collecting $50 a passenger for its role in promoting several charter flights to Europe each year. In high tourist season, there often was more than one flight every month. Most of the flights carried at least a hundred members of the Mechanics', many of whom had never been inside the building. The membership soared to an unprecedented twelve thousand, more than twice normal. Where else could you get that kind of a travel discount for $6 in annual dues (or even $10)?

In the mid 1970s the balloon popped. There had been a frightening sell-off in the stock market in 1974. Air traffic was growing, and the pressure to raise airfares grew with the demand. The Airline Deregulation Act of 1978 dealt a mortal blow to the business of bargain charters. The Mechanics' Institute, like hundreds of other clubs, museums, churches and alumni associations that had profited from the affinity charter system, lost that source of revenue and the allure for new members. The swollen membership of the Mechanics' declined to its historic level, below seven thousand. In any case, the revenue from members' dues had never covered the cost of running the library. There had to be income from donations, bequests, investments, rents—anything clean and legal.

For a few years the trustees worked with a local travel agency to offer packaged tours to Europe or South America for groups of fifteen or twenty; but the complexity and uncertainty of the travel business, the fierce competition for customers and the disappointing return ended that experiment. In the end, the trustees turned to their wealth in real estate to strengthen the financial position of the Institute—and to finance a major revitalization project for 57 Post Street, which was reaching the venerable age of seventy.

San Francisco's Department of City Planning was working at that time on a master plan to guide the growth of the downtown district. An important and politically controversial aspect of the plan was a scheme to protect landmarks from demolition by permitting the property owners to realize a gain by selling some of the unusable development potential of the space. The novel plan, developed in studies by San Francisco Architectural Heritage (then named the Foundation for the Preservation of San Francisco's Architectural Heritage), was so new that it required an educational course for city officials.

Dean Macris, then the director of planning, recalled a meeting convened by Mayor Dianne Feinstein and the planning staff to convince City Attorney George Agnos of the feasibility and the legality of transferable development rights (TDRs)—basically, shifting rights to construct a building from one property owner to another in a different location.

"Several ashtray stands, which at the time adorned the Mayor's office, were moved about in an effort to explain how the transfer of development rights would work," Macris wrote in an article published by SPUR, the San Francisco Planning and Urban Research Association. "The debate was intense. The Mayor became convinced and urged Agnos to withdraw his objection to this critical element of the [downtown] plan, which he ultimately, and reluctantly, did."

In October, 1982, the trustees of the Mechanics', having concluded that the construction of a high-rise building at 57 Post Street was unlikely because of the small size of the lot and the sentiment in the city favoring curbs on downtown density, approved the sale of transferable development rights for fourteen stories of overhead space to San Francisco Federal Savings for $1.6 million.

It was the first of several sales of TDRs by the Mechanics'. These transactions, as preservationists hoped, assured the long-term protection of a historically and architecturally significant building. They also contributed significantly to the financial endurance of such valuable institutions as the Mechanics'. The TDR sale created the basis for an endowment fund that would allow the Institute to continue its full services in a time of declining revenues.

The rattling eighties

WON'T THIS CITY
EVER CALM DOWN?

1980 The $38.5 million Louise M. Davies Symphony Hall opens with a week-long series of concerts in September conducted by Maestro Edo de Waart. On the final evening, Mrs. Davies, the principal benefactor, plays the triangle with a group of fellow patrons of the symphony on drum, rattle and several bird-whistles.

1981 Director Wayne Wang, born in Hong Kong and educated in the Bay Area, produces his first feature-length movie, a black-and-white 16mm film called *Chan Is Missing*, a quirky, unsentimental look at San Francisco's Chinatown, which had previously been depicted as a place of mystery, menace and sing-song chatter.

1982–83 The boom in high-rise office buildings in the "financial triangle" scratches the sky with new towers: One Montgomery Street, 101 California Street, Shaklee Terraces at 444 Market Street, the Federal Reserve Building on lower Market Street and the Montgomery Building at 456 Montgomery Street.

1984 The NFL 49ers, powered by quarterback Joe Montana, have their greatest season (15 wins, one loss) and make their second of five trips to the Super Bowl, where they wipe out the Chicago Bears 23–0.

1986 Advocates of restrictions on downtown development, after several tries, push through a voter initiative—Proposition M—to place a permanent cap on additional office space.

1987 Randy Shilts publishes *And the Band Played On*, the first book-length journalistic account of the effects of the imported AIDS virus upon San Francisco's large community of homosexual men— an epidemic that was officially ignored or denied until the devastating death rate, first observed by public health physicians in 1981, at last began to cause widespread concern.

1988 The San Francisco Public Library closes its business branch on Kearny Street at Sacramento in a cost-cutting step to avoid duplication of expensive business publications that are also available at the Main Library in Civic Center.

1989 A 15-second earthquake on the San Andreas Fault, measuring 7.1 on the Richter magnitude scale and centered 60 miles south of San Francisco, strikes at 5:04 P.M. on October 17, just as game three of the World Series between San Francisco and Oakland is about to begin at Candlestick Park.

1989 Amy Tan publishes her autobiographical novel *The Joy Luck Club*, the first intimate account of family life in Chinatown since Jade Snow Wong's *Fifth Chinese Daughter* in 1950.

CROCKER GALLERIA, a pedestrian corridor with three levels of boutiques and small cafés under a barrel-vaulted glass roof, brought a fresh presence to Post Street, directly across from the Mechanics' Institute, in 1983. In this view from the fourth-floor members' lounge of the Mechanics' Institute, the charming roof garden atop the 1908 banking hall at the corner of Post and Montgomery looks like a tiny park lost among the faceless walls of surrounding towers.

STARTING AGAIN, AGAIN

FIFTY-SEVEN POST STREET, like most buildings in the downtown financial district, suffered only minor damage from the Loma Prieta earthquake. The small number of patrons and staff members who were in the Mechanics' Library that evening heard a terrifying, grinding sound, saw falling books, felt lurching floors, and, afterward, shared an overwhelming sense of relief and gratitude for a sound old building blessed with durable materials, honorable construction and solid subsoil.

Throughout the downtown district, the work of repair was relatively swift. Business as usual resumed as soon as people regained confidence to move around. But for most of the Bay Area, left with a crippled transportation system, massive costs of replacing lost property, curtailed public services and a painful decline in income from tourism, the task of reconstruction dragged on for several years.

During the period of reconstruction, the Mechanics' Institute suffered several years of inertia, internal dissension and loss of direction, the sort of institutional stasis that occurs in the history of many long-lived institutions. Some of the problems grew out of intramural and intensely personal disagreements on policy and management.

At the beginning of the decade, however, it appeared that the Mechanics' was moving forward. The sale of transferable development rights in the 1980s had created a reserve of capital with which to build a growing endowment fund. The library and Chess Room were serving a near-record 6613 members, including more than 1200 life members. In this heady environment, the board agreed to an ambitious goal of $2 million for improvements to the building, computerization of the library and a "large meeting room" for classes, lectures, films and other events. In January, 1992, the library staff began the task of entering some 150,000 items from the card catalogue into a computer index base accessible to all users of the library.

During the second half of the decade, however, the rise and abrupt fall of the dot-com industry in northern California had a powerful impact upon commercial rents in downtown San Francisco. Rental income, which had once been the Mechanics' most reliable asset, became a questionable resource. At almost the same time, the portion of the Institute's endowment that was invested in equities lost value and income in the crash of an overblown stock market.

Faced with declining membership and curtailed revenue, the staff and trustees of the Institute pushed ahead with a series of projects to improve the quality of the rental spaces, better serve the members, resume a diversified program of events and classes—and balance the budget. Approaching age one hundred fifty, the Mechanics' put aside recriminations and regrets and began, step by step, to prepare for the future.

AFTER THE LOMA PRIETA QUAKE soldiers from the Presidio and cordons of yellow tape restrained looters, as well as distraught survivors, from entering ruined buildings like this house in the Marina District. Although the quake was less severe and destructive than the 1906 disaster, it took sixty-three lives (largely in the collapse of a two-tiered freeway in Oakland), injured almost four thousand and caused an estimated $10 billion in damage to property. In San Francisco, half a dozen major public buildings, including City Hall, the Opera House and the Civic Auditorium, sustained costly damage. Four freeways were closed, and two notorious eyesores—the Embarcadero Freeway and its connector to the Bay Bridge—were later demolished, to the relief and delight of many San Franciscans. Also gone was the accursed Cypress Viaduct in the East Bay, where forty-two motorists died.

A FIRESTORM, FINE ARTS AND A DOT-COM FRENZY

1991 The forty-one-day Persian Gulf War forces Iraqi invaders out of Kuwait but leaves dictator Saddam Hussein in control of Iraq.

1991 The Eureka Theatre, a small resident company in a 250-seat house in the Mission District, commissions and presents the world premiere of "Millennium Approaches," the first part of Tony Kushner's two-part drama *Angels in America*. The Broadway production of Kushner's epic of sexual, racial, social, religious and political conflicts wins a Pulitzer Prize and a Tony Award in 1993.

1991 A devastating firestorm, driven by hot October winds, ravages 1600 acres in the residential hills of Oakland and Berkeley, destroys 2449 single-family homes and more than 430 apartment units, injures more than 150 people and kills 25. Damage is estimated at $1.5 billion.

1992 The American premiere of John Adams's *The Death of Klinghoffer* brings a controversial view of Middle Eastern terrorism to the San Francisco Opera.

1994 The historic Presidio army base, established as a colonial outpost by Spanish soldiers in 1776, is decommissioned and transferred to the National Park Service, adding the last large segment to the 75,000-acre Golden Gate National Recreational Area, America's first great urban national park.

CANDLESTICK PARK officially became "3Com Park," for the 3Com Corporation of Marlborough, Massachusetts, which purchased five years of naming rights in 1995. In 2002, the fickle stadium resumed its maiden name for a couple of years, then took the title "Monster Stadium" for its new patron, Monster Cable Products of Brisbane, California.

1994–95 The so-called Internet Age begins in Silicon Valley—the San Francisco–Stanford–San Jose corridor—with the founding of Netscape by Marc Andreesen and Jim Clark in April, 1994. About fifteen months later, Jeff Bezos launches the Amazon.com Web site in Seattle. For the next five years, the proliferation of Internet start-up companies lifts the real estate market in downtown San Francisco and the South of Market district to unrealistic (and untenable) heights before the whole dot-com industry implodes with hundreds of casualties.

1995 The 49ers go to Super Bowl XXIX in Miami, Florida, where quarterback Steve Young posts a 49–26 win over San Diego.

1995 Poet Robert Hass, a professor in the English department of the University of California, Berkeley, and a Stanford University doctorate, becomes the first Poet Laureate ever appointed from the Western United States.

1995 The San Francisco Museum of Modern Art (SFMOMA), on January 18, the sixtieth anniversary of its founding, welcomes 10,000 people to the opening of its dazzling new building on Third Street, designed by architect Mario Botta.

1995 Guitarist Jerry Garcia, fifty-three, San Francisco–born founder of The Grateful Dead rock group of the "Flower Power" era, dies of a heart attack at a rehabilitation hospital near his home in Marin County.

1996 San Francisco's first African American mayor, the veteran California legislator Willie Brown Jr., is inaugurated at City Hall.

1996 The $14 million New Main Library, a Baroque-Modern fusion building by the architectural partnership Pei Cobb Freed, opens at Civic Center. Almost immediately, critics say there's not enough space inside for books.

1997 The most volatile stock market in memory drops 554 points (Dow-Jones average) in one day, and then makes its largest one-day gain the next day, with 1.1 billion shares traded.

1997 Stanley B. Prusiner, professor of biochemistry in the School of Medicine of the University of California, San Francisco, wins the Nobel Prize in medicine for his discovery of prions – "a new biological principle of infection."

1998 Lawrence Ferlinghetti, in a speech accepting appointment as the city's first poet laureate, decries the effects of automobile congestion, gentrification, chain stores, Internet start-up companies and other recent aspects of urban life upon the historic texture and pleasant idiosyncrasy of San Francisco.

1999 The Hearst Corporation buys the city's oldest and largest newspaper, the *San Francisco Chronicle*, from its owning family, descendants of M. H. de Young, who co-founded the paper in 1865. Hearst then sells its own daily *Examiner,* flagship of the newspaper chain started by William Randolph Hearst in 1887.

2000 Pac Bell Park (later renamed SBC Park) a retro-style, 40,000-seat baseball stadium at the edge of the bay, opens for its first season as the home of the National League San Francisco Giants.

2003 The Asian Art Museum, now the largest in the United States devoted exclusively to the arts of Asia, relocates (March 20) to a new and larger home—the former Main Library at Civic Center, refurbished with major support of Chong-Moon Lee, a Korean American technology entrepreneur. The renowned Avery Brundage collection, augmented by numerous purchases (including $1 million in Korean art funded by Mr. Lee) is the core of the 15,000 items.

2004 The San Francisco Giants' Barry Bonds hits his 661st home run, topping the record of his godfather, center fielder Willie Mays, who hit a career total of 660 home runs before his retirement in 1973.

HOW TO CHANGE WITHOUT CHANGING

I have always thought that the Mechanics' Institute was—and has remained to a great extent—an unchanging institution.

—Joseph A. Moore, president
of the Institute, 1969–74

PRIDE, TRADITION and conservative financial management served the Mechanics' Institute well for most of its history. But in the decade of the 1990s, the venerable old library, the handsome old building and the traditional old customs of operation were wearing out. The library lacked space to increase and update its holdings. The building needed such fundamental work as new elevators, new rest rooms, extensive electric cabling and a more reliable system of fire protection. At the same time, the Institute was faced with a revolution in the way people receive and transmit information, entertainment and education. The Mechanics' Institute, if it was to survive, would have to apply the new infor-

mation technology to its own operations—and also find a way to win the attention and participation of a changing constituency, distracted by the overwhelming abundance of images and words.

In the exhilarating atmosphere of the early 1990s, the board moved ahead on its announced program to modernize the building and the library. Between 1994 and 2000, the Institute spent close to $1.2 million on such major projects as elevators, sprinkler systems and a meeting room and lounge for members.

Despite the collapse of the financial market, which depressed the value and income of the endowment fund, the board continued in a yearly, pay-as-you-go commitment to the building and the library—another $1 million in capital projects, culminating in a $290,000 installation of moveable shelving to permit the expansion of the library to 200,000 volumes.

During this period of growth, the board and staff worked on a new mission statement describing the purposes of the institution. After many rambling discussions, rough drafts, additions and deletions, on March 22, 1999, the board adopted a few sentences pledging the Mechanics' Institute "to provide a center for cultural and educational advancement"—and agreeing to maintain a library of circulation and reference, to sponsor educational and cultural programs and to operate a Chess Room.

Left to be answered were difficult questions that never would have occurred to the little group of ambitious craftsmen who established the Institute in 1855. Is there a need for a membership library in the financial district of a commuter city? How can its role be differentiated from that of other educational and cultural institutions? Should it aspire to be a sort of educational community center? Or, should it hew to the line it has always followed, of providing an inexpensive, non-exclusive, club-like refuge for people who seek the companionship, stimulation and solace of books?

Implicit in the trustees' mission statement was a recognition that this "unchanging institution" might be required to adapt and change in many ways, but that the Mechanics' Institute would continue to offer unique value to the Bay Area community, and that books, ideas, images and written words, and the sort of people who cherish them, would continue to be found in places like the Mechanics' Institute.

MOVEABLE SHELVES, demonstrated by Librarian Inez Shor Cohen, add storage space in the basement to bring the library to its historic level of 200,000 books.

HIGH TECHNOLOGY
AMID TRADITION

THE TRANQUILITY of the Mechanics' Library, with its comfortable, club-like atmosphere, belies the vitality of a thriving educational and cultural institution that serves about 5000 subscribing members on five floors of its downtown headquarters. Year-round, the library offers opportunities for study, entertainment and literary appreciation. Members sign up for classes in the use of electronic databases and the Internet; book discussion groups; or workshops in creative writing, play writing and poetry. Many use the library for access to essential reference sources, both print and electronic. Some 600 chess players—and many visiting challengers—participate in tournaments, demonstrations, tutorial lectures and pick-up games. Special events, most of which are open to the public, include poetry readings, classic cinema, documentary films, seminars in finance and culinary arts, wine and food tasting and 50 guest appearances each year by authors of new fiction and nonfiction, history, biography, science, technology, social and political issues and economics.

IN THE STREET-FLOOR LOBBY, a volunteer docent shows visitors the ceiling-high mural *The Arts*, painted by Arthur F. Mathews in 1917.

OPEN SHELVES of reference books and specialized journals, computer terminals served by vast databases, racks of current periodicals—and a trained librarian on duty to offer guidance to the collections—give the third-floor Reference Room the feeling of a superbly equipped personal workspace.

"THE WAY A LIBRARY SHOULD LOOK"

"THE MECHANICS' INSTITUTE LIBRARY looks the way a library should look," says the *SF Weekly*. "The setting is hushed, pristine and ambient with brass rails, burnished wood, comfortable armchairs, and the pleasant smell of a used bookstore." More than three-quarters of the Institute's members borrow fiction, nonfiction, audio books, videos, DVDs and other materials from the open stacks and cupboards. An uncounted number use noncirculating materials in the second- and third-floor reading rooms or consult the eleven electronic databases available to the library's subscribers.

e) and among the open shelves, professional interests and research staff helps researchers use materials. Many members enjoy interesting book to take home. wed that most of today's ble, graphic designers, s.

THE MYSTERY BOOK CLUB gathers for its monthly brown-bag lunch in the fourth-floor board room. What did you think of this month's book? At what point did you identify the killer? What are we reading next? Dorothy L. Sayers? Graham Greene? P.D. James? Shirley Jackson? After three years of sharing insights and criticisms, the mystery readers, like other interest groups, have grown into a close affiliation within the larger community of the Mechanics' Institute Library.

READERS, WRITERS AND LEARNERS find like-minded people of various ages in the Mechanics' book groups. The Library limits the size of each group, gives members priority in joining and welcomes suggestions for new groups. Currently, there are workshops for poets, playwrights and fiction writers; an "intergenerational" reading group; a series of seminars on California history and literature facilitated by authors and historians; and a Proust Society that is making its way, year after year, through *Remembrance of Things Past.*

CHESS CHAMPIONS like the Institute's Grandmaster-in-Residence Alex Yermolinksy (above) coach advanced players as well as beginners with lectures, demonstrations and grandmaster tournaments. Russian-born Yermolinsky, a chemist, was U.S. Champion in 1996 and has written many articles and several books on chess. Among other champion players from the Bay Area who have contributed to the fame of the Mechanics' Club are Grandmaster Nick de Firmian, winner of three U.S. championships, and Australian-born Walter S. Browne of Berkeley, a six-time U.S. Champion. Both rank high in the 100 strongest players in the United States. De Firmian and Browne played major roles in securing for San Francisco the prestigious Pan Pacific International Grandmaster tournaments, hosted by the Mechanics' in 1987, 1991 and 1995.

WOULD-BE CHAMPIONS learn the fundamentals at weekday summer school and year-round weekend classes. Many learners attend Mechanics' tournaments for advanced players, juniors and women. Among the strong players who started young at the Mechanics' were Art Wang, Gil Ramirez and the late Carroll Capps. A young player (above left) ponders a printed problem under a framed picture of world champion Bobby Fischer. Other students joust with a chess-playing computer (above), while experienced players (below left) are absorbed in their own informal game.

AN EVENING FOR THE BOOK

A STAGED READING by the talented performance group Word for Word draws an overflow audience to an evening members' meeting in the fourth-floor café-lounge. Other popular events include Friday night showings of classic American and foreign films, book-signings, and illustrated lectures on gardening, technology, photography, science, travel and, of course, money.

BEFORE THE SHOW, actors review their roles in the multi-character dramatic reading of a short story by Alice Munro (above), while trustees, subscribers and members of the public meet and chat at the refreshment bar.

A SMILING AUDIENCE hangs on every word of tonight's reading by polished professionals. Other popular programs like Bastille Day, Poetry Month, the Documentary Film Salon and the ritual Bloomsday Reading from James Joyce's *Ulysses* require advance reservations, as do events that involve collaboration with other cultural and educational organizations such as the San Francisco Opera, American Conservatory Theater, Magic Theater, World Affairs Council, Japan Society, Asia Society and Strybing Arboretum. Independent bookstores— City Lights, Stacey's and A Clean Well-Lighted Place for Books—cooperate in handling book sales at appearances by local or touring authors.

BEST SEATS are free to members of the Institute at nearly all events. A low ticket charge (usually $5 to $7) encourages non-members to attend daytime and evening programs, but late-comers must sometimes endure obstructed vision.

PRIZE-WINNING JOURNALIST HERB CAEN drew a record crowd to a members' meeting on December 12, 1984, when he was at the peak of his influence as a newspaper columnist. The popular success of Caen's provocative mixture of humor, nostalgia and inside information created innumerable rivals and imitators for sixty years, none of whom lured away his devoted following. Many San Franciscans believed that a single item—or, better, frequent mention—in Caen's column guaranteed success (or failure) to a restaurateur, retailer, entertainer or politician. His rare public appearance at the Mechanics' Institute reflected his admiration for the historic institution he had once called "San Francisco's best-kept secret."

ATTORNEY NEIL FALCONER and Ewelina Krubnik, fifteen, play a demonstration game in the main reading room. Falconer began playing at the Mechanics' in 1938, while he was a student at University High School in Oakland. A trustee since 1973, he has twice been president of the board. Ms. Krubnik, a high school student, has been studying chess at the Mechanics' since she was eight.

INDEX

Note: An italic page number indicates an illustration.

PRODUCED BY
WILSTED & TAYLOR
PUBLISHING SERVICES

PROJECT MANAGEMENT
Christine Taylor

PRODUCTION MANAGEMENT
Jennifer Uhlich

PRODUCTION ASSISTANCE
Andrew Patty

COPYEDITING
Nancy Evans

DESIGN
Melissa Ehn and Tag Savage

PRINTER'S DEVIL
Lillian Marie Wilsted

INDEXING
Janet Vail

PRINTING AND BINDING
Regal Printing Ltd., Hong Kong,
through Stacy Quinn of Quinnessentials
Books and Printing, Inc.

The Mechanics' Institute, a membership library, chess club and adult education center,
welcomes friends and new subscribers to visit us at 57 Post Street
(between Kearny and Montgomery Streets), San Francisco, CA 94104,
or telephone (415) 393-0105 or worldwide web: www.milibrary.org.